W9-ATO-328

WAR·TIME

ALSO BY MARY L. DUDZIAK

Exporting American Dreams: Thurgood Marshall's African Journey

Legal Borderlands: Law and the Construction of American Borders (coeditor)

September 11 in History: A Watershed Moment? (editor)

Cold War Civil Rights: Race and the Image of American Democracy

War·Time

An Idea, Its History,
Its Consequences

MARY L. DUDZIAK

OXFORD
UNIVERSITY PRESS

Amazon 4/2013   20.87

OXFORD
UNIVERSITY PRESS

Oxford University Press, Inc., publishes works that further
Oxford University's objective of excellence
in research, scholarship, and education.

Oxford   New York
Auckland   Cape Town   Dar es Salaam   Hong Kong   Karachi
Kuala Lumpur   Madrid   Melbourne   Mexico City   Nairobi
New Delhi   Shanghai   Taipei   Toronto

With offices in
Argentina   Austria   Brazil   Chile   Czech Republic   France   Greece
Guatemala   Hungary   Italy   Japan   Poland   Portugal   Singapore
South Korea   Switzerland   Thailand   Turkey   Ukraine   Vietnam

Copyright © 2012 by Mary L. Dudziak

Published by Oxford University Press, Inc.
198 Madison Avenue, New York, NY 10016

www.oup.com

Oxford is a registered trademark of Oxford University Press

All rights reserved. No part of this publication may be reproduced,
stored in a retrieval system, or transmitted, in any form or by any means,
electronic, mechanical, photocopying, recording, or otherwise,
without the prior permission of Oxford University Press.

Library of Congress Cataloging-in-Publication Data
Dudziak, Mary L., 1956–
War time : an idea, its history, its consequences / Mary L. Dudziak.
    p.   cm.
Includes bibliographical references and index.
ISBN 978-0-19-977523-1 (hbk. : alk. paper)
1. War. 2. War (Philosophy.) 3. Time—Philosophy.
4. Time—Social aspects—United States.
5. United States—History, Military—21st century.
6. United States—History, Military—20th century.
I. Title. II. Title: Wartime, an idea, its history, its consequences.
U21.2.D75   2012
355.020973—dc23   2011026311

9 8 7 6 5 4 3 2 1

Printed in the United States of America
on acid-free paper

To Bill and Alicia

*WAR consisteth not in battle only, or the act of fighting;
but in a tract of time, wherein the will to contend by
battle is sufficiently known; and therefore the notion of
time, is to be considered in the nature of war.*
—*Thomas Hobbes*, Leviathan

CONTENTS

WAR·TIME

Introduction

WHAT KIND OF TIME IS a "wartime?" In war, regular time is thought to be interrupted, and time is out of order. During World War I, soldiers synchronized their watches before heading into combat. Yet battle became an extended present, as considerations of past and future were suspended by the violence of the moment. In the trenches, the historian Eric J. Leed has written, "the roaring chaos of the barrage effected a kind of hypnotic condition that shattered any rational pattern of cause and effect," so that time had no sequence. And so one meaning of "wartime" is the idea that battle suspends time itself.[1]

War also breaks time into pieces, slicing human experience into eras, creating a before and an after. It marks the beginning of one historical period, and the end of another, so that the historian Cheryl A. Wells writes that the American Civil War "split nineteenth-century American time into two discrete units," antebellum and postbellum.[2] Once historical time is divided, war is thought to occupy a certain kind of time. Wartime.

Yet wartime is more than a historical signpost, a passive periodizer, and therefore is not only the province of historians. It is thought to function as an abstract historical actor, moving and changing society and creating particular conditions of governance. The Roman philosopher and statesman Cicero's ancient saying, "In time of war, law is silent" (*inter arma silent leges*), is regularly invoked for the proposition that law and politics differ during wartime.[3] Wartime becomes a justification for a rule of law that bends in favor of the security of the state. Traditionally, this distortion has been tolerated because wars end. In the twenty-first century, however, we find ourselves in an era in which wartime—the war on terror—seems to have no endpoint. This generates an urgent problem in American law and politics: how can we end a wartime when war doesn't come to an end?

This book takes up the idea of wartime and its effects, showing that a set of ideas about time are embedded in the way we think about war. In particular, we tend to assume that wartime is always followed by peacetime, and therefore that an essential aspect of wartime is that it is temporary. The assumption of temporariness becomes an argument for exceptional policies, such as torture. And those who cross the line during war sometimes argue that circumstances deprive them of agency; their acts are driven or determined by time.

Assumptions about the temporality of war are embedded in American legal and political thought. It is as if time were a natural phenomenon with an essential nature, shaping human action and thought. But our ideas about wartime clash with our experience of twenty-first-century war, revealing that a confusion about *time* obscures our understanding of contemporary war.

Much attention has been paid in recent years to wartime as a "state of exception," but not to wartime as a form of time. For the Italian political philosopher Giorgio Agamben, a state of exception "is a suspension of the legal order itself," marking law's boundaries.[4] Viewing war as an exception to normal life, however, leads us to ignore the persistence of war. If wartime is actually normal rather than exceptional time, then law during war must be seen as the form of law we usually practice, rather than a suspension of an idealized understanding of law.

This book takes up the different ways that ideas about time affect our understanding of war. The chapters do not follow a conventional narrative history of war, but instead examine how war and time are imagined. The focus is on the concept of wartime and its consequences.

This is not a merely academic enterprise, however. My aim is to illuminate a conundrum: we imagine wars to be bound in time, but the American experience is to the contrary. Since 9/11, war has been framed in a boundless way, extending anywhere in the world that the specter of terrorism resides, even as some of the country's political leaders—on the left and right—denounce its seeming endlessness. This book cannot explain how to bring war to an end, of course, but it can help to illuminate the way confusion about war and time helps to enable our politics of war.

Chapter 1 examines ideas about time itself. We tend to think of time as a feature of the natural world, but our understanding of time is part of the culture of our age. Wartime, like other kinds of time, does not have an essential nature, but is a product of culture and history. We tend to believe that there are two kinds of time, wartime and peacetime, and history consists of moving from one kind of time to the next. Built into the very essence of our idea of wartime is the assumption that war is temporary. The beginning of a war is the opening of an era that will, by definition, come to an end. When we look at the full time line of American military conflicts, however, including the "small wars" and the so-called forgotten wars, there are not many years of peacetime. This shows us that war is not an exception to normal peacetime, but instead an enduring condition.

Chapter 2 takes up a major war of the twentieth century, World War II. We assume we know when this war "happened," from the shock of Pearl Harbor—a "date which will live in infamy," as President Roosevelt called it—to the excitement of V-J day captured in an iconic photograph of a sailor kissing a nurse in New York's Times Square. But this war is harder to place in time than we think, as the legal consequences bled out beyond these iconic moments, and there were not one but many endings to the war, spanning a period of years. Still, our memory of World War II remains encapsulated between certain dates, and this informs our ideas about what real war is.

The Cold War, the focus of chapter 3, is an era of ambiguity when the foundation was laid for the American national security state. Even the title "Cold War" is contradictory, suggesting an era of war-but-not-war. Military engagement during this period did not fit the model of American wartime, as the United States faced off in a decades-long conflict with the Soviet Union, and American leaders debated whether the country was in a permanent state of war. In retrospect, however, many have worked to fit the era into preexisting conceptual categories of wartime and peacetime. In this way, an era that foreshadows the current experience of ongoing war is instead seen as an example of an old-fashioned, time-limited wartime.

As war spills across the time line of American history, attempts to confine it have emerged in memory and narrative, through the war stories that are passed down from one generation to the next, and that are performed in feature films and documentaries. Yet war narratives come not only from personal experiences but also from the public relations side of American national security. Public diplomacy has been a feature of all important twentieth-century American military conflicts. The American government's need to rally support for military action and to encourage public support for military engagements in faraway lands that appear to have little impact on daily life at home has been central since at least the Korean War. During the "war on terror," as chapter 4 discusses, the role of war-related public relations was especially important as the Bush administration largely succeeded in framing the post–September 11 era as a wartime. At the same time, the narrative cohesion of American wartime was eroding. In cases relating to Guantánamo detainees, Supreme Court justices first attempted to fit the era into the traditional and confined understanding of wartime. But ultimately, anxiety about ongoing war led them to question executive branch policies more closely.

My aim throughout is to critique the way that the concept of wartime affects thinking about law and politics, but not to argue that *war itself* has no impact. One reason that wartime has so much power in framing history is that the outbreak of war is often perceived as ushering in a new era. The onset of war is seen, however, not as a discrete event, but as the beginning of a particular era that has temporal boundaries on both sides. I do not wish to question the power of catalytic moments like the Japanese attack on Pearl Harbor, but rather to call attention to the way such events produce a set of assumptions about their endings.[5]

This book focuses on American thinking about war and time. This is not because the American experience is "exceptional" or more significant than the histories of other regions of the world, but instead because it is simply a reasonable starting place for a historian of the United States. A more global and comparative account would benefit from collaboration with others. And Americans have a particular need to understand their role in this history. It is American drones, after all, that hover in the airspace of nations we are not formally "at war" with. The U.S. role in worldwide conflict makes it essential to unpack American thinking about wartime, and the way it affects the politics of war.

This history enables us to see that there is a disconnect between the way we imagine wartime, and the practice of American wars. Military conflict has been ongoing for decades, yet public policy rests on the false assumption that it is an aberration. This enables a culture of irresponsibility, as "wartime" serves as an argument and an excuse for national security–related ruptures of the usual legal order. If we abandon the idea that war is confined in time we can see more clearly that our law and politics are not suspended by an exception to the regular order of things. Instead, wartime has become normal time in America. Because of this, the politics we have during this time are our normal politics. The American people cannot wait for a new peacetime to end detentions at Guantánamo or to rein in expanded presidential war power. Time itself will not wash them away. Wartime has become the only kind of time we have, and therefore is a time within which American politics must function.

President Barack Obama has called our own day "an age without surrender ceremonies," and yet we continue to believe that wartime comes to an end.[6] We are routinely asked to support our troops, but otherwise war requires no sacrifices of most Americans, and as conflict goes on, Americans pay increasingly less attention to it. Troops may be deployed to an unfamiliar corner of the world, and we see occasional headlines about drone attacks or civilian casualties, but war has drifted to the margins of American politics. Even the killing of Osama bin Laden brought the war in Afghanistan only briefly into focus. Demystifying the idea of wartime, and revealing how it works in American culture, will not end any wars or even get Americans to care more about them. But it might offer a path toward a more satisfactory understanding of the relationship between war and American democracy.

1

What Time Is It?

IN CLEVELAND, OHIO, WAR TIME began at the circus. On the evening of February 8, 1942, Cleveland's mayor, Frank J. Lausch, ceremoniously advanced two clocks, following the evening performance of the Grotto Circus. In doing so, he brought Cleveland's time into sync with year-long Daylight Savings Time, which was called "War Time." The mayor told the circus crowd, in an address broadcast on the radio, that the change in time was "'gratifying' because of the electricity it would save for war work." Around the country, time changed at 2:00 a.m. Standard Time on February 9, in compliance with a new federal law establishing ongoing daylight saving time as an energy-saving measure during World War II. Meanwhile Clevelanders shared ideas about how to spend the "invisible hour which vanished when clocks shifted from 2 a.m. to 3 a.m." Among the more tasteful suggestions was "visiting the wife's relatives."[1]

This change brought greater uniformity to a diversity that continued to persist in the United States. Mechanical clocks came to America with the first European settlers in the seventeenth century, but on their own clocks could not impose consistency in time. In the nineteenth century, towns often set their clocks by the sun, so that communities not far from each other had clocks set at different times. This created havoc for railroads and other businesses, leading to efforts to make time practices more uniform, ultimately leading to the creation of four time zones in the United States. During World War I the federal government attempted to standardize time by codifying these time zones, but simultaneously sanctioned a departure from "standard time." Daylight Saving Time (DST) was imposed as a war-related energy-saving measure during the spring and summer. After the war, Congress repealed DST, but some states and localities adopted it as a local matter.[2]

Even though clock time pervaded American culture during the 1920s and 30s, the clock did not make time uniform, even within particular regions. Instead, there was a jumble of local times as some communities used daylight savings time and others did not. This meant that, as Congressman Luther Patrick of Alabama put it, you could drive from Washington, DC, to Birmingham, Alabama, through Chattanooga, Tennessee, "and you can get to Chattanooga before you get to Knoxville [Tennessee], which you have already passed." Some longed to bring rationality to temporal chaos. "It is not the question of whether we rise at 5 o'clock in the morning or at 6 o'clock," A. Julian Brylawski, vice president of the Motion Picture Theater Owners of America, remarked. "The real fact is that this daylight saving being in effect in a spot here and a spot there, being on different times, merely upsets our conception of time."[3]

In August 1941, War Time came back when Congress convened hearings on Daylight Savings Time as a defense matter. Leland Olds, chairman of the Federal Power Commission, predicted that defense needs alone could require as much as one hundred billion kilowatt hours per year of electricity. Since use of electricity for all purposes was 145 billion in 1940, anticipated war needs would require diverting to defense a large amount of power used for civilian purposes. During 1941, the United States was already experiencing power shortages for defense industries. Meanwhile,

Germany had vastly increased its power capacity, taking over power plants in Norway, France, and Poland, countries Hitler had overrun.[4]

The greatest energy savings from daylight saving in the United States would not come from factories, since defense-related plants were operating 24-hours per day. Instead, it would come from "a change in the habits of all people; in the domestic use of electricity as well as a commercial use." But the total expected power saved would only be between 1 and 5 percent per year. One reason a national requirement of daylight saving would have such a limited effect was that many states and cities had already adopted it for the spring and summer months. Olds argued that this seemingly small amount was nevertheless needed to ease communities through power surges without disrupting military production. Still, the minimal effect on power coupled with the widespread impact on American communities shows that War Time's most significant function was not in energy-saving, but in engaging Americans directly with their nation's war efforts. Like creating Victory Gardens and buying War Bonds, calibrating daily life to Daylight Saving Time—War Time—was a tangible way for ordinary Americans to serve their nation. Alarm clocks in the dark morning hours were a constant reminder that the nation was at war.[5]

Standard time itself was a human construct, but for many Americans it seemed natural or God-given, and they objected to giving it up. The Oklahoma State Senate passed an anti–Daylight Saving Time resolution, insisting that "it is the sun and not the laws of man that determines daylight and darkness." Farmers opposed daylight saving, and their concerns illustrate that tensions over War Time stemmed from the ways clock time had come to be experienced as an essential element of culture. The timing of much farm work was dictated by the sun, but Hugh F. Hall of the American Farm Bureau Federation argued that Daylight Saving Time had "shortened the workday on the farm, particularly with respect to the day which can be used at harvest time." The reason was that clocks had become tools of daily living. Farmers used them to conduct business "because the shop-keeper and the merchant and the railroads and the greater segment of the population are operating in accordance with the clock, which, in turn, is operated according to daylight-saving time." One farmer's frustration was evident in a constituent letter read into the record by Congressman Joseph P. O'Hara of Minnesota at hearings on an unsuccessful repeal bill in 1944:

> To delude one's self that it is 6 o'clock when the sun, moon and stars and God in heaven have ordained that it is but 5 o'clock, I believe justifies the . . . statement that the so-called daylight saving time probably stands at the head of the list as an example of complete asininity.[6]

Fred Brenckman, Washington representative of the National Grange, objected on behalf of dairy farmers who would have to get up at 3:00 a.m. rather than 4:00 a.m. to milk their cows. They "must work in harmony with natural law or they work to no purpose at all," he insisted. But nature had not changed, only the name of the hour they had to rise.[7]

Back in Cleveland, ironically one of the first reactions to Daylight Saving Time was to turn on the lights. The *Cleveland Plain Dealer* announced that city street lights would now stay on until 7:14 a.m. Eastern War Time.[8]

WARTIME AS A FORM OF TIME

Just as Americans changed their clocks during World War II, we adjust ourselves to a different order of time during war. Wartime is not merely a regulation of the clock; it is the calibration of an era. Once we enter it we expect the rules to change. Some burdens are more tolerable because we think of war as important and exceptional, and also because, by definition, wartime comes to an end.

World War II Daylight Saving Time did not succeed completely in bringing uniformity to the nation's mix of time practices, but one moment brought the country together. December 7, 1941, the day the Japanese attacked Pearl Harbor, was seen almost immediately as dividing time into different eras. It created a before and an after, just as the Civil War divided nineteenth-century American history, and the twentieth century is thought to be segmented into periods of wartime and peacetime, with World War I and World War II as the essential time markers. History after 1945 is often called "postwar," even though war continued in Korea, Vietnam, and elsewhere.[9] Yet the onset of war is not seen as a discreet event, but as the beginning of a particular era that has temporal boundaries on both sides, so that entering a "wartime" is necessarily entering a temporary condition. Built into the concept of wartime is the assumption of an inevitable endpoint.

The opposite of wartime is of course peacetime, and history is thought to consist in the movement from one kind of time to another. Much depends on what time it is: the relationship between citizen and state, the scope of rights, the extent of government power. A central metaphor is the pendulum—swinging from strong protection of rights and

Wartime/Peacetime

wartime	peacetime	wartime	peacetime

weaker government power during peacetime to weaker protection of rights and stronger government power during
wartime. Moving from one kind of time to the next is
thought to swing the pendulum in a new direction.[10]

Dividing time into wartime and peacetime offers a con-
venient way to periodize history, but more is at stake in
our constructions of wartime. Law is thought to vary
depending on what time one is in. Despite Cicero's *inter
arma silent leges*, law is not completely silent during wartime, but it is generally assumed to be different, with
courts affording less protection to civil liberties and giving
more deference to executive power. The controversy tends
to focus on the questions of whether the balance between
rights and security in a particular war context was the
right one, and whether departures from peacetime rules
are useful or regrettable.[11]

Wartime is assumed to be temporary, but now we find
ourselves in an era when American political leaders announce
an end to hostilities—"mission accomplished"—but war continues.[12] War's tendency to defy time boundaries has a longer
history, as we will see in later chapters. But how is it that time
boundaries have become a feature of the way we think about
war? The ideas that wartime and peacetime are distinct eras

seem as natural and inevitable as did Standard Time to World War II–era American farmers. How might American history look if we understood wartime and peacetime as cultural features, as self-made categories, as constructs?

"Time feels like an essential and defining feature of human life," the historian Lynn Hunt explains, but we rarely stop to think about it. "Like everyone else," she writes, "historians assume that time exists, yet despite its obvious importance to historical writing—what is history but the account of how things change over time?—writers of history do not often inquire into the meaning of time itself." One of the difficulties in talking about time is that the words we use to describe it seem to presuppose a particular understanding of it. "When pressed to define it, we inevitably fall back upon duration, change, and ultimately, the tenses of our languages, past, present, and future."[13]

Ideas about time are rooted in culture, but as the sociologist Emile Durkheim suggested in *The Elementary Forms of Religious Life* (1912), we have trouble examining this. "We cannot conceive of time," he wrote, "except on condition of distinguishing its different moments." If we "try to represent what the notion of time would be without the processes by which we divide it, measure it or express it with objective signs, a time which is not a succession of years, months, weeks, days and hours! This is something nearly unthinkable." But Durkheim was curious about how these categories came into existence. "What is the origin of the differentiation?" he asked. Where do we get the categories that time is divided into? Durkheim helps us to see that minutes and hours are not features of the natural world. They come from social life, he argues, from the ideas we share that help make our world understandable.[14]

One common idea about time is that it is linear. Linearity is thought to be natural and inevitable, and is sometimes contrasted with a cyclical view of time. The anthropologist Carol Greenhouse suggests that we tend to think of non-linear time as an aspect of traditional cultures. Forms of time thought to flow from cultural contexts are often referred to as "social time." This is contrasted with "our" time—linear time—that is thought to exist in nature.[15]

But even linear time has a history, and can be understood within a cultural context, Greenhouse argues. Linear time is also social time. Greenhouse finds the origin of linear time in Jewish and Christian tradition: "first, the origin of time in creation and, second, the end of time in a day of judgment." Time's linearity comes from "the geometric connection between these two end points." Secular understandings of time are often hazy about the nature of origins and endpoint, but retain this linearity. Once time is thought of as a progression from one point to another, other assumptions follow. For Greenhouse, referring to linear time means referring to the image of time as an "irreversible progression of moments, yielding ordinal conceptions of past, present, and future as well as duration."[16]

Culture does not flatten time into one set of ideas, however. Instead, Greenhouse argues, competing conceptions of time overlap and compete for ascendancy. Initially, in the West, a linear understanding of time competed with indigenous European ideas that time was a pendulum, moving between binary oppositions (day/night, summer/winter). The dominance of linear time comes about because it is useful to us, Greenhouse argues, "not because it is the only 'kind' of time that is culturally available. The meanings of linear time are inseparable from its cultural history of use."[17]

Ideas about time are sometimes tied to the experience of modernity. Building on the work of the influential British historian E. P. Thompson, historians have examined the way that clock time brought time-discipline to labor, aiding development of the factory system. Developments in science, technology, business, and global affairs have affected the role of time. The creation of the telegraph and laying of transcontinental telegraph cables were important steps, leaving "no interval of time between widely separated places proportionate to their distances apart," said one enthusiast in 1886. But this shift was disconcerting. When people communicated across great distances, different parts of the day—noontime, nighttime, and morning—coincided. Even within a region, the clock did not impose uniform time, for localities had their own times, usually set to the sun. Reformers hoped that world "standard time" would bring predictability, since differences in clock time flummoxed railroad schedules and military campaigns. The railroads led the effort to put standard time into effect, dividing the United States into four different time zones. Then, representatives from twenty-five countries met in Washington, DC, in 1884 at the Prime Meridian Conference, dividing the world into twenty-four time zones, including the four time zones now used in the United States. A common chronology of years had existed since the Late Middle Ages, but wide variations remained in the division of time into smaller units. An International Conference on Time in 1912 tried, unsuccessfully, to rationalize a calendar that remained chaotic. Two years later a German businessman proposed a system to divide the year into the particular weeks and months we now follow. Meanwhile, in the 1890s, a machine was invented that could stamp an employee's card when the worker entered and left the shop. "Punctuality and the recording of work time did not originate in this period," the historian Stephen Kern writes, "but never before had the temporal precision been as exact or as pervasive as in the age of electricity." Once time was viewed as uniform and governed by the clock, it helped create what the historian Benedict Anderson called an "imagined community," as clock time helped knit together a common sense of national identity. Americans don't know what all their fellow citizens are doing at any moment, but they have "complete confidence in their steady, anonymous, simultaneous activity." The nation is conceived as "a solid community moving steadily down (or up) history."[18]

But is time the same for everyone? The literary scholar Thomas M. Allen suggests that the sameness of time that is supposed to come from our use of clocks, watches, and calendars "is only possible if technologies produce time by themselves." To understand time, we must ask how people used these devices, and why they wanted them. We can then see, Allen argues, that the idea of a homogeneous national time "begins to shatter into myriad fragments of heterogeneous, local, and transient temporal cultures." Just as we might experience politics or art differently—we might look at the same painting but derive different meanings from it—we can experience time differently even as we look at the same clock. But heterogeneity does not result in chaos. Our differences, according to Allen, "are themselves the threads out of which the fabric of national belonging has long been woven." The idea of the heterogeneity of time helps us to see that, in Allen's words, time is not "a transhistorical phenomenon, an aspect of nature or product of technology existing outside of human society." Instead, it is

produced by human beings working within specific historical circumstances.[19]

Just as clock time is based on a set of ideas produced
not by clocks, but by the people who use them, wartime
is also a set of ideas derived from social life, not from
anything inevitable about war itself.

THE IDEA OF WARTIME

Wartime is important to American law and politics, but, as
with other ways of categorizing time, we don't tend to
inquire about it. We treat it as if it were a distinct feature of
our world, as if warfare brought with it a particular temporality. The impact of this way of categorizing time on our
thinking tends to go unexamined.

War structures time, as does the clock. Stephen Kern
argues that World War I displaced a multiplicity of "private
times," and imposed "homogenous time," through an "imposing coordination of all activity according to a single
public time." In the context of war's public time, individual
differences remained. The defense production worker's day
was regimented by the factory schedule; the parent whose
child was at war marked time from one letter to the next; a
soldier's life was marked by the immediacy of combat, and
by long periods of waiting. These very different personal
experiences with time played out under a common umbrella:
the trajectory of war from beginning to end.[20]

When the outbreak of war is a dramatic attack, the way
Pearl Harbor was experienced, it brings the nation together,
so that a widely dispersed population feels that they have
experienced the same thing at the same time, bringing about

Anderson's consciousness of simultaneity. Because the attack is on the nation, and it is the nation that mounts a response, this moment of simultaneity also helps bind the people to the state, the source of their defense. It is in war that citizens see the state, the progressive writer Randolph Bourne wrote in an essay published after his death in 1918. At other times "the State is reduced to a shadowy emblem which comes to consciousness only on occasions of patriotic holiday."[21] It is also in war that we encounter the state in time, or that we grant the state an expanse of time: a wartime.

Once war has begun, time is thought to proceed on a different plane. There are two important consequences of this shift: first, we have entered a time that calls for extraordinary action, and second, we share a belief that this moment will end decisively, so that this shift is temporary. Because of this, built into the idea of wartime is a conception of the future. To imagine the future requires an understanding of the past.[22] In wartime thinking, the future is a place beyond war, a time when exceptional measures can be put to rest, and regular life resumed. The future is, in essence, the return to a time that war had suspended.

An era is sometimes presented as simply a compendium of time. In teleological histories, an era might be a stage in societal "progress." An era of wartime, in contrast, is more than a passive time marker. It can determine history. During the French Revolution, for example, Lynn Hunt suggests that "a new kind of voluntarism" opened up, and with it the idea that "human will could consciously shape the future." This coexisted with "a new kind of determinism." For example, Bertrand Barère, a leading member of the Committee of Public Safety, and viewed as a driving force behind the Reign of Terror, "excused his actions as the product of his time." According to Hunt, Barère claimed that he did not shape his revolutionary epoch. Instead he "only did what I had to do, obey it." Barère's time, he argued, "sovereignly commanded so many peoples and kings, so many geniuses, so many talents, wills and even events that this submission to the era and this obedience to the spirit of the century cannot be imputed to crime or fault."[23] In American wartime thinking, there is also a powerful sense of determinism. Actions that would normally transgress a rule of law are seen as compelled by the era, as if commanded by time. And, as did Barère, individuals defend themselves by arguing that their actions were compelled or justified by the times.

Time is a critical framing device in international law, Oren Gross and Fionnuala Ní Aoláin argue in their book, *Law in Times of Crisis*. "The main traditional feature of the international legal system is its dichotomized division between times of peace and wartime, with the former constituting the norm and the latter the exception to that norm." Wartime is also a central category in domestic American law and politics. Scholars as well as policymakers tend to see wartime as a historical actor, having force in history, enhancing the power of the government and sometimes compromising rights. The legal scholar Geoffrey Stone argues in *Perilous Times: Free Speech in Wartime* that wartime results in incursions on freespeech rights. The history of law during wartimes serves as a warning, in the hope that leaders in future wartimes might get the correct balance between individual rights and security. As do most legal scholars, Stone views wartime as exceptional. The federal government "prohibits political dissent *only* in wartime," he writes.[24]

Twentieth-Century American Wartimes
(as commonly represented in scholarship on rights and wartime)

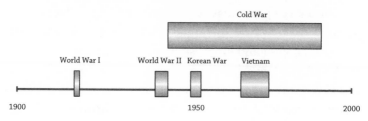

For Stone, the World War I years offer a particularly powerful example of the United States government's tendency to overreact and repress liberty during war. For example, the Supreme Court upheld the Socialist Charles Schenck's conviction under the Espionage Act of 1917, which, among other things, criminalized conspiracy "to cause insubordination . . . in the military and naval forces of the United States." The "conspiracy" of Schenck and his Socialist Party companions involved distributing leaflets calling for resistance to the draft and urging draftees to protect their constitutional rights. Justice Oliver Wendell Holmes wrote the majority opinion, upholding Schenck's conviction. In a famous passage, he argued that the nature of free speech rights differed depending on when they were invoked: "When a nation is at war many things that might be said in times of peace are such a hindrance to its effort that their utterance will not be endured so long as men fight and that no Court could regard them as protected by any Constitutional right." *Schenck v. United States* (1919) is widely cited as a case about what happens to rights during wartime.[25]

Congress passed the Sedition Act of 1918 during World War I—"the most repressive legislation in American history," according to Stone. The Act criminalized statements that were thought to endanger the war effort, including "disloyal, profane, scurrilous or abusive language about the form of the government, the Constitution, soldiers and sailors." The only Sedition Act case to reach the Supreme Court was *Abrams v. United States* (1919), involving Russian immigrants who protested the war by throwing leaflets off rooftops and out windows. The Supreme Court upheld their conviction, this time prompting an important dissent by Holmes and Louis Brandeis. Holmes retained the idea of war's temporality in *Abrams*, as he and Justice Brandeis began a series of dissents that would become central to First Amendment jurisprudence. Government power "undoubtedly is greater in time of war than in time of peace," Holmes wrote. "But, as against dangers peculiar to war, as against others, the principle of the right to free speech is always the same."[26]

Civil liberties violations during World War I are, for Stone and other scholars, evidence of wartime's deleterious impact on American law. During wars there has been "a mood of fear and anxiety that can readily explode into intolerance and vigilantism," he writes, and political leaders "went out of their way to inflame these responses by promoting a climate conducive to repression." This history is of great importance, but we must look more closely at the way wartime works as a framing device for scholars of civil liberties. Frames are "principles of selection, emphasis, and presentation composed of little tacit theories about what exists, what happens, and what matters," writes the sociologist Todd Gitlin. The wartime frame offers not only a description of the past, but also an implicit theory about what happens to rights in American history. It works to restrict our study of the impact of war and militarization within certain exceptional moments, making it harder to see the ways that war has become part of the normal course of American life.[27]

War's exceptionality is important to Stone's argument in *Perilous Times*. He contrasts wartimes with peacetimes, which are thought of as the normal times that are breached by war, and calculates that peacetime makes up "roughly 80 percent of our history." These peacetimes are largely absent from the narrative, however. But war is only exceptional during the twentieth century if we ignore the numerous American "small wars" carried on in Haiti, the Philippines, and elsewhere. And in Stone's own account, war is seamless from the onset of World War II through Vietnam. The idea of discrete wartimes continues to do important work for civil liberties scholars well into a century during which the dividing lines between war and peace became so much more difficult to see.[28]

RECOGNIZING WARTIMES

A common way to place a war in time is to rely on the date it was declared and the date an armistice was signed. But the last time the United States declared war was during World War II. All military engagements since then, and many before it, happened without the benefit of a congressional declaration. Since World War II, congressional ratification of military action and funding for wars have often been seen as the functional equivalent of a formal declaration, as with the Vietnam-era Gulf of Tonkin Resolution, but this often happens after military action is under way.[29]

Various definitions of war tend to compound the difficulty. Definitions of "wartime" tend to be circular. According to *The Oxford Essential Dictionary of the U.S. Military*, a wartime is "a period during which a war is taking place." Definitions of "war" itself have changed over time. In the *Prize Cases* during the Civil War, which involved the legality of Lincoln's blockade of the South in the absence of a formal declaration of war, the U.S. Supreme Court defined war as simply "that state in which a nation prosecutes its right by force." Traditionally, an essential component of a definition of war was that it was between states. But the state has dropped out of prominent attempts to define war. For example, *The Oxford Companion to American Military History* defines war by referring not to violence between nations, but to "organized violent activity, waged not by individuals but by [people] in groups." Similarly, the Australian scholar Hedley Bull wrote in *The Anarchical Society* that war consists of "organized violence carried on by political units against each other." Violence, by itself, is not war "unless it is carried out in the name of a political unit." The involvement of the state affects the legitimacy of a conflict, but not whether it is a "war." Bull's capacious definition of war contrasts with the more narrow way in which war is often defined in international law, for only war between states is thought to be lawful and legitimate. "Sovereign states have sought to preserve for themselves a monopoly of the legitimate use of violence." Ambiguity in the definition of war reinforces the ambiguity in the definition of wartime.[30]

Definitions of war have turned on the nature of adversaries and their objectives, but whether the population affected by a conflict thinks there is a war also turns on the weapons used. Troops and machine guns, for example, are obvious signifiers of war, but by the middle of the twentieth century airpower was more central to the question of whether military activity seemed like a war. By the early twenty-first century, catastrophic bombing, in itself, did not signal war's presence—the 1995 Oklahoma City bombing was not thought to be warlike—but the use of airplanes in the September 11 attacks helped fuel the feeling that the nation was at war.[31]

The timeline of American warfare looks more precise if we turn to indicia of war known better to American soldiers: eligibility criteria for combat-service medals and membership in American veterans' organizations. These criteria cause wartime to swallow much of American history. For collectors of United States military campaign medals, "America's military history encompasses much more than the major conflicts of the Revolutionary War, Civil War, World War I, World War II, Korean War and the Vietnam War," write John E. Strandberg and Roger James Bender in their catalog of American military medals. "Some of our nation's early heroes emerged from battles in Cardenas, Cuba; Peking, China; Port-au-Prince, Haiti; or Bluefields, Nicaragua." As Strandberg and Bender put it, "these 'little wars' helped define America as a world military power."[32]

Military medals and ribbons, retired Marine Corps Lieutenant Colonel Thomas A. Richards has written, "give a snapshot" of an individual's service: "where a person served, what he or she has done, and how the person did it." While medals for valor, like the Silver Star, honor acts of bravery, campaign service medals simply recognize meritorious service during a particular military campaign. From the beginning, the small wars were central to campaign service medals. Major General Adna R. Chaffee proposed federal military campaign medals while commanding American forces in China during the Boxer Rebellion in 1900. The first

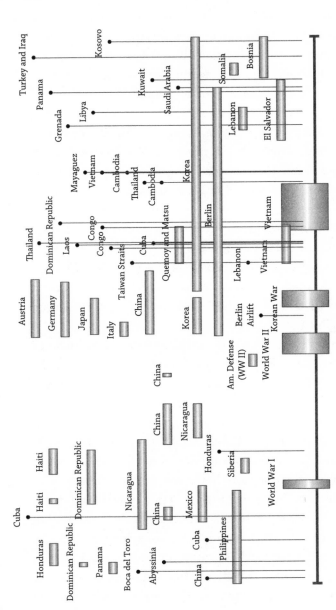

This chart includes nearly all twentieth-century U.S. Armed Services campaign medals described in John E. Strandberg and Roger James Bender, *"The Call of Duty": Military Awards and Decorations of the United States of America*, 2nd ed. (San Jose, CA: R. Bender Publishing, 2004). Campaign medals are not medals for valor but are for participation in various military campaigns. Medals were excluded from the chart if they did not involve operations against armed opposing forces or military occupation. When operations involved conflict with an organized social group, rather than the military forces of another nation, such conflict fits within contemporary definitions of warfare and is included. A full list of campaign service medals appears in the Appendix.

medals were announced by the War Department in 1905, and reached back to commemorate service in the Civil War, wars against American Indian tribes, the Spanish-American War, and military action in the Philippines and China.[33]

Small wars have been regularly honored by the American military even though, as a 1940 Marine Corps training manual noted, "small wars" is "a vague name for any one of many a great variety of military operations." A Nicaraguan Campaign medal, for example, recognized Navy and Marine Corps actions in August 1912, when approximately 2,400 Americans aided government forces allied with the incumbent president, captured one of his opponents, and forced the other into exile. A disputed election also led to the Mexican Campaign, with over 100,000 National Guard troops joining 15,000 U.S. Army troops to battle Pancho Villa from March 1916 to February 1917. American troops who served were eligible for medals.[34]

Membership in veterans' organizations also includes these little wars. The Veterans of Foreign Wars was established in 1899 after the Spanish-American War. The organization honors service in many twentieth-century military engagements, including China (1900–1901), Cuba (1906–1909), and Mexico (1911–1915). For the organization Disabled American Veterans (DAV), membership criteria turn on whether a veteran was "disabled in line of duty during time of war." "Time of war" is defined to include many twentieth-century conflicts, including Haiti in 1915. For DAV eligibility, one long era of war existed from 1940 to 1976, covering World War II, Korea, Vietnam, and other conflicts. The only non-war period after World War II, other than a period of seven months in 1990, was from October 15, 1976, to November 4,

1979. The American Legion, a veterans' group with 2.6 million members established in 1919, is more discriminating. Prospective members must have served in one of only seven conflicts, however they include small wars in Lebanon, Grenada, and Panama.[35]

In the smaller conflicts recognized by veterans groups and honored with military campaign medals, American military personnel traveled to other nations with their military units, wearing uniforms and bearing arms. Following their commander-in-chief's orders, they engaged in hostilities. These sorts of actions fall within most definitions of war, though they tend to be ignored in the great narratives of American wartimes. And they don't figure in accounts of the impact of war on American law and politics. It is only through forgetting the small wars that so much of American history is remembered as peacetime.

The name for small wars in the British experience is the wars of empire. Americans are less comfortable with the idea that their nation has an imperial history, but the use of military might to, in essence, govern vast stretches of the globe has been a feature of all global powers in the last century. The laws of war traditionally focused only on wars between states. The wars of empire fell outside the law; they were instead matters of imperial governance. The experience of battling indigenous groups over territory and sovereignty has also been part of American history. Military action against American Indian tribes was included among the first wars for which American soldiers could be awarded campaign service medals, and American troops battled against an independence movement for control of the Philippines after the Spanish-American War, a bloody military campaign that lasted for years.[36]

Latin America and the Caribbean were sites of many American military engagements. It was in Latin America, the "workshop of empire," the historian Greg Grandin writes, that the nation developed both the ideology of an "empire of liberty," and the "tactics of extraterritorial administration" leading to an approach to imperial power that was "better suited for a world in which rising nationalism was making formal colonialism of the kind European nations practiced unworkable."[37] Latin America and other sites of small wars were also workshops of American war strategy, aiding the development of the counterinsurgency methods that have gained currency today.

These smaller-scale battles are erased from the memory of American wars. This is not only because the wars of empire fell through the cracks of the law of war at the time. It is also because, as Amy Kaplan argues, Americans have had a strong desire to forget their imperial history, so that until recently, the idea of American empire "was considered a contradiction in terms, . . . hurled only by left-wing critics."[38] In American memory, the nation's wars are large-scale battles against evil, and not small wars in pursuit of less grand ambitions.

What happens to the idea of wartime when the rest of American war is remembered will be taken up in the pages that follow.

2

When Was World War II?

IN THE SUMMER OF 1949, John Lee was behind prison bars, fighting for his life. A brutal murder led to his imprisonment at the United States Army Disciplinary Barracks at Camp Cooke in California, but Lee's fate would be determined by a curious question: when did World War II end?

Lee and three other incarcerated soldiers were charged with attacking and killing another inmate, Charlie Taylor, on June 10, 1949. Their weapons were knives made from pipes and other materials at hand. The men were convicted following a court-martial and sentenced to death. There was just one difficulty. Article 92 of the Laws of War provided that "no person shall be tried by court-martial for murder or rape committed within the geographical limits of the States of the Union and the District of Columbia in time of peace." Whether the court-martial was lawful turned on whether the date of the crime, June 10, 1949, was wartime or peacetime. Lee brought a habeas corpus challenge, arguing that it was a time of peace, depriving the court-martial of power over the case. The prosecution disagreed, arguing that "peace, in the complete sense, has not been declared in connection with the recent hostilities against the Empire of Japan and Germany."[1]

Lee's first run-in with the military justice system was in March 1945, when he was court-martialed for stabbing "a negro [sic] in the chest with a bayonet." He was sentenced to five years in prison, but the sentence was suspended on August 14, 1945, the date Japan announced its surrender.

Lee returned to service, but soon after, while absent without leave from the U.S. Army in Europe, he was arrested for armed robbery. He overpowered military police officers and escaped, and he then became, according to the subsequent Board of Review, "a member of a notorious terroristic gang of AWOL's in Paris," and was recaptured after the U.S. military, Paris police, and civilians gave chase, with gunfire resulting in what Parisians called the noisiest day in the city since liberation. Ultimately Lee was prosecuted and incarcerated at Camp Cooke, where he continued to commit acts of violence.[2]

The current location of Vandenberg Air Force Base, Camp Cooke was established in an agricultural area along the coast in northern Santa Barbara County, California, in 1941 as part of a major build-up on the West Coast in anticipation of U.S. entry into World War II. The isolation of the base from settled areas made it an ideal location for an intercontinental ballistic missile site in later years. During World War II, Camp Cooke trained soldiers bound for the front lines. A prison was established at the base for Italian and German prisoners of war. With large numbers of trainees at the camp, a stockade was also needed for American soldiers charged with offenses. Eventually this became the United States Disciplinary Barracks, thought of as the army's most modern prison, usually housing 800 to 1,500 inmates. The majority of them, in the army's view, were "not criminals but boys 'who got themselves in trouble in the Army.'" The army's objective was to rehabilitate them and release them to civilian employment or to restore them to duty in the armed services.[3]

But John Lee was not simply a boy who got in trouble with the army. "During the war we took in all kinds of men,"

Captain Edward H. Montgomery later recalled. "Some of them were criminals," and some even "joined the Army as an alternative to a prison sentence." When Charlie Taylor was murdered, Lee struck no blows himself, but he helped orchestrate it. Witnesses claimed that afterward Lee was overheard saying "We got that dirty *** and we'll get the rest of them," and "This isn't the first man I've killed and it won't be the last."[4]

It was unclear whether "racial feeling" played a role in the killing—the assailants were white and the victim was black—although Camp Cooke authorities reported Taylor was probably killed "because he was a negro [*sic*]." But the legal issue in the case was literally whether the date of the crime was during wartime or peacetime. The defense argued that "since the war has been over for some time and there has been a cessation of hostilities, 'peace' did in fact exist," so a court-martial was unlawful. On appeal after Lee's conviction, however, the Board of Review took judicial notice of the fact that "at the time of and prior to trial in this case Congress had by appropriate declarations proclaimed a state of war to exist between the United States and other specified countries, and also, that at the time of trial, peace had not been officially proclaimed nor had treaties of peace with all nations with which a state of war existed been ratified." Hence, it was not a "time of peace," so that the court-martial had proper jurisdiction over the case.[5] Lee's petition for habeas corpus would ultimately place before the United States Supreme Court the question of what kind of time it was when Charlie Taylor was murdered.

World War II is thought of as having obvious starting and ending points: an abrupt beginning at Pearl Harbor and a clear end when the Japanese surrendered after the United

States dropped atomic bombs on the cities of Hiroshima and Nagasaki. These iconic moments provide a frame for many history books, and often mark the boundaries within which social scientists collect data on the war's impact. But as *Lee v. Madigan* shows, even World War II is hard to locate firmly in time. The story extends beyond these dates, and scholars miss the war's full impact when they exclude from consideration U.S. engagement with this global conflict prior to the events of December 7, 1941, and after surrender documents were signed. World War II is an example of the way American war spills beyond tidy time boundaries.

The effort to contain World War II within the Pearl Harbor-to-surrender frame reinforces traditional ideas about wartime. This matters because wartime is the occasion for the use of the federal government's war powers. The assumption that wars are finite legitimizes the exercise of war powers by making it seem that their use is temporary. War powers have not, however, been confined within dates of declared wars. They often precede it and survive an armistice, so that the dates of a declared war don't determine the span of government power.

The problem in *Lee v. Madigan* of when war ended had arisen before. During the Boxer Rebellion in China, Private Fred Hamilton was sentenced to life at hard labor for the killing of Corporal Charley Cooper at Camp Reilly, Peking, China, on December 23, 1900. Hamilton appealed his conviction, arguing that there was no jurisdiction under the laws of war, because a court-martial was only appropriate "in time of war, insurrection or rebellion." The case turned on whether a state of war existed on the date of the crime. There had been no declaration of war between the United States and China, yet the court found that a state of war existed "by reason of the occupation of Chinese territory by the large military force of this government, under authority of the Department of War," the skirmishes between U.S. and Chinese troops, and the fact that Congress was paying the "officers and men of this government there engaged on a war basis." The jurisdiction of the court-martial was sustained by the Supreme Court in 1919.[6]

Hamilton's case was relied on in *Ex parte Johnson*, in which a lower court in 1925 dismissed a similar challenge to a court-martial of a soldier who was in the state of Chihuahua, Mexico, under the command of General John Pershing, to pursue Pancho Villa. Similarly, in *United States v. Ayers*, the U.S. Court of Military Justice held that a "time of war" existed in Korea in December 1950, in spite of the absence of a declaration of war. In *United States v. Anderson*, the U.S. Court of Military Justice held that the United States was in a "time of war" in Vietnam on November 3, 1964, for the purpose of the offense of desertion in violation of Article 85, Uniform Code of Military Justice, even though war in Vietnam was never formally declared.[7]

Lee v. Madigan would seem to be more straightforward, since the relevant war—World War II—had been declared. The case would turn on the question of when that war ended. What were the possibilities? Germany surrendered on May 8, 1945. Japan announced its decision to surrender on August 14, 1945, and surrender documents were officially signed on September 2, 1945. From these events, it would seem clear that the war was over in 1945, as we usually assume. But the cessation of hostilities was not declared by President Truman until December 31, 1946, and even then he noted that "a state of war still exists." If a state of war continued, then what had changed to justify a cessation of hostilities? It was "in the public interest to declare, that hostilities have terminated," the president suggested, but even as late as 1951, "as a legal matter," the nation was still in a state of war against Germany. Truman didn't call for an end to this state of war until July 1951, but also stressed that this would not affect the occupation of Germany. A peace treaty with Japan went into effect on April 28, 1952, although its restrictive terms left the nation "free, yet not free," as the *New York Times* put it.[8]

The various endings to World War II left the Supreme Court in something of a muddle. And Congress made it murkier, terminating some Articles of War in 1947, but not all. Article 92, allowing the death penalty for murder but forbidding trial by court-martial during peacetime, was not repealed. Because it remained in effect, the government argued that the nation was "not then 'in time of peace' for the purpose of Article 92." In an earlier case, *Ludecke v. Watkins* (1948), the Court held that ending a state of war was a "political act," and courts must defer to the judgment of other branches. In *Ludecke*, a German national was detained after Germany had surrendered, but a peace treaty had not yet been signed. The German prisoner contended that the president's war powers did not "survive cessation of the actual hostilities," and so he should be released. The Court found, however, that "war does not cease with a cease-fire order, and power to be exercised by the President . . . is a process which begins when war is declared but is not exhausted when the shooting stops."[9]

The end of war was a political question, the Court in *Ludecke* put it, not a question for judges who did not have the "technical competence or official responsibility" for this. Similarly, *Woods v. Cloyd Miller* (1948) concerned a

WHEN WAS WORLD WAR II? | **39**

rent-control act passed in 1947, after the fighting had ended, and addressing a *post*war housing crisis. A Cleveland landlord raised the rent for his tenants by 40 to 60 percent, and was sued by the federal government under the new statute. The district court in *Woods* struck down the act, finding it to be unconstitutional. On appeal, the landlord argued that if war powers were not contained within a narrowly defined wartime, they would be too broad, since "the effects of war under modern conditions may be felt in the economy for years and years." But the Supreme Court upheld the statute, finding that there was a "direct and immediate" relationship between the housing crisis and war, so Congress's war power had been properly invoked. The war power "does not necessarily end with the cessation of hostilities," Justice William O. Douglas wrote for the Court, but "includes the power 'to remedy the evils which have arisen from its rise and progress' and continues for the duration of that emergency." Prohibition laws were upheld after World War I under a similar rationale.[10]

But these cases did not drive the Court's decision in *Madigan*, Justice Douglas, again writing for the majority, argued. "Congress in drafting laws may decide that the Nation may be 'at war' for one purpose and 'at peace' for another." The Court's job was "to determine whether 'in the sense of this law' peace had arrived." While in *Woods* the Court found the war powers to extend long beyond the dates of surrender, *Madigan* concerned "a grant of power to military tribunals to try people for capital offenses," unlike the regulatory powers at issue in the rent control case. Assuming that Congress was "alive to the importance" of constitutional guarantees to a fair trial when it enacted Article 92, Douglas gave the Article a "common sense" reading, holding that the date of the crime was a "time of peace" as those words were used in the Article. In spite of the nod to *Ludecke*, he tried to wring out of Article 92 a reading that comported with his view of common sense.[11]

The Court's ruling freed John Lee from prison, which may have disturbed law enforcement. The Court's opinion would not be remembered as a landmark, however. By 1959, when *Madigan* was decided, the porous nature of the boundaries of the war power was an ongoing feature of American jurisprudence. Alongside the seamlessness of war powers in American law, however, the idea that wars are bound in time continued to animate American culture in popular accounts of the "good war."[12]

FIRING THE FIRST SHOT

In contrast with the murkiness of World War II's ending, its beginning would seem to be clearer, with the attack on Pearl Harbor seared in American memory as the beginning of World War II. But the historian Waldo Heinrichs has written that the war "crept up, stage by stage, over many years."[13] World War II is often regarded as the last time in U.S. history that war powers were properly contained within a declared war, but the beginning of the war illustrates an enduring dynamic: the use of executive branch war-related powers outside of a declared war.

Through the late 1930s, as conflict broke out in Asia and Europe, Americans remained isolationist, focused more on the economy and New Deal policies. But, concerned about German aggression, Roosevelt moved to increase

American arms production and sought unsuccessfully to repeal American neutrality laws after Hitler invaded Czechoslovakia in March 1939. He often bypassed Congress and drew on his commander-in-chief powers to fight what the constitutional scholar Edward Corwin called "the war before the war." In the absence of a declaration of war, Roosevelt sought to make the nation an "arsenal of democracy," supplying war materiel to American allies. He began these efforts years before Pearl Harbor. The ultimate result, Corwin argues, is that "a 'shooting war' was precipitated without Congress having been consulted."[14]

In early 1938 the president issued an executive order enabling the army to give older weapons to private contractors, who could then sell them abroad. Eventually, a committee was established to better coordinate these foreign military purchases. Roosevelt was concerned that the Neutrality Acts, passed after World War I, hampered the nation's ability to support France and England. Support for European allies was critical to national security, for if Europe fell to the Nazis, North America would be increasingly vulnerable. Congress eased restrictions in the Neutrality Act of 1939, enabling "cash and carry" sales during hostilities.[15]

By late summer 1939, "the imminence of war in Europe overshadowed everything else in importance," Robert Jackson, then U.S. solicitor general, wrote in his memoir. As war was declared in Europe, Roosevelt found himself in a difficult situation. "The President was under the peculiar difficulty, all the time, that if he made any move that looked like getting the country ready for war, he was charged with being a warmonger," Jackson recalled. But the president nonetheless "felt obligated to take some steps that would prevent us from being caught unawares." Roosevelt devised a dual policy of peace and simultaneously preparing for war. "Each step that he took in favor of one of those policies was construed as an abandonment, or perhaps as insincerity, concerning the other."[16]

After the Nazi blitzkrieg in Europe and Japanese advances in Asia in the spring of 1940, "almost overnight the 'free security' enjoyed by the United States since the Napoleonic Wars disappeared," Heinrichs writes. "The Atlantic was no longer a friendly ocean: Hitler controlled the far shore." Roosevelt responded by increasing arms production. Although the president remained restricted by Neutrality Acts, Congress passed a military draft bill, and the president called up the National Guard. When France fell to the Germans in the spring of 1940, Roosevelt drew on his 1938 executive order, sending weapons and ammunition to the British. On June 15, 1940, as Germany expanded its reach, Roosevelt signed a resolution enabling the secretary of war to authorize the manufacture or procurement of war materiel "on behalf of any American republic," a step toward what the legendary journalist Arthur Krock called "hemispheric solidarity" throughout the Americas. On September 3, 1940, the president announced that he had entered an agreement with Britain to lend them aging American ships, in exchange for their willingness to lease British bases to the United States. At this time, Roosevelt did not seek congressional involvement in the deal, and did not propose a treaty with Britain on the matter, as that would have required Senate ratification. Jackson justified the move as being within the president's foreign affairs

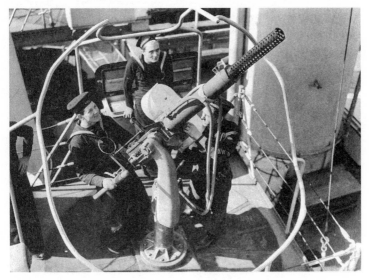

British sailors try out a gun on board one of the first of fifty U.S. destroyers sent to England under a bases-for-destroyers exchange deal that President Roosevelt negotiated with England in 1940 without the involvement of Congress. October 4, 1940. Bettmann/CORBIS.

power, and his power as commander-in-chief of the armed services.[17]

Meanwhile, at home foreign espionage increased markedly. Attorney General Frank Murphy reported on June 30, 1939, that in the previous year the Justice Department had pursued four Espionage Act prosecutions, involving at least twenty-three defendants, while only two such cases had been tried in previous years since the First World War. One case involved eighteen German spies charged with stealing U.S. Army, Navy, and Defense Department secrets. Fourteen escaped before they could be apprehended. Another German was convicted for photographing weapons and weapons sites in the Panama Canal Zone. The impact of national security on the work of the Justice Department would only increase. For the 1940 fiscal year, Robert Jackson, who replaced Murphy as attorney general, began his report with National Defense, noting that the department dealt with many defense-related matters that year, and "the effect of needs of national defense is reflected in practically every division and bureau of the Department." By June 1941, Jackson reported that the Department of Justice had rapidly expanded, "due chiefly to the war abroad and to the national defense program." Meanwhile, the Criminal Division reported that as of June 1940 "the European conflict and the present unsettled condition of world affairs has resulted in increased activity and investigative work in connection with espionage, sabotage, neutrality, and kindred activities." The department was also working to safeguard civil liberties, however, for "in times of national defense it is necessary that the basic democratic principles such as freedom of speech and of the press be maintained." The Criminal Division's docket "increased materially" the next year, with "the greatest single accretion" relating to national defense.[18]

Congress responded to increased concern about security in 1940, amending the Espionage Act of 1917 and increasing its penalties, and passing the Smith Act, requiring aliens to register with the federal government and prohibiting conspiracies to advocate the overthrow of the United States government. (The Act would be used more extensively to prosecute members of the Communist Party during the Cold War era.) President Roosevelt sought increased federal surveillance power, successfully promoting wiretapping authority for the FBI and other investigatory bodies.

As the perceived need for domestic surveillance increased, the role of the FBI expanded, and by late 1941, the historian David Reynolds argues, "many features of what would emerge as the 'national security state' were already apparent in embryo."[19]

Following his election to an unprecedented third term in 1940, Roosevelt addressed national security more directly. "At no previous time has American security been as seriously threatened from without as it is today," he warned in his State of the Union Address, January 6, 1941. The country had an immediate need for "a swift and driving increase in our armament production," as war materiel was needed by the United States and its allies. Roosevelt also gave the global conflict a moral dimension. The United States would seek to secure "four essential human freedoms" everywhere in the world: freedom of speech and expression, freedom of worship, freedom from want, and freedom from fear. It would be a "moral order," and "the very antithesis of the so-called new order of tyranny which the dictators seek to create with the crash of a bomb."[20]

By the spring of 1941, the political winds had shifted such that the president finally felt he could involve Congress more directly in war planning. On March 11, Congress passed the Lend-Lease Act, enabling more extensive support to U.S. allies. The Act empowered the president to provide war materiel "for the government of any country whose defense the President deems vital to the defense of the United States." Allies would not pay for equipment with cash, but instead by returning it or by using it in the war effort. Roosevelt likened it to lending a neighbor a hose to fight a fire. The Act was fiercely opposed by isolationists. Senator Robert Taft argued that it would "give the President power to carry on a kind of undeclared war all over the world, in which America would do everything except actually put soldiers in the front-line trenches where the fighting is." After its passage, the president escalated American involvement in what the *New York Times* called "the Battle of the Atlantic," opening American ports to British ships in need of repair from German bombs and torpedoes. On March 29, he ordered seizure of sixty-five ships in American ports belonging to Axis and occupied nations.[21]

Meanwhile, on March 15, Roosevelt again addressed the global threat at a White House Correspondents Dinner, making clearer the implications for American security. "Nazi forces are not seeking mere modifications in colonial maps or in minor European boundaries," he warned. "They openly seek the destruction of all elective systems of government on every continent—including our own." In order to prevail against this threat, the nation would "have to make sacrifices." This extended to every citizen. "Whether you are in the armed services; whether you are a steel worker or a stevedore; a machinist or a housewife; a farmer or a banker; a storekeeper or a manufacturer—to all of you it will mean sacrifice in behalf of country and your liberties."[22]

As Hitler continued to advance in Europe and North Africa, and German battleships made forays near Iceland in the North Atlantic, conditions seemed more dire than ever. Roosevelt raised the stakes in an address on May 27, 1941, emphasizing the need to block Germany from establishing bases in the Atlantic that could be stepping stones in an attack on the Americas. He made it clear that, if provoked, the United States would respond with force. Roosevelt proclaimed an unlimited public emergency. "The war is approaching the brink of the Western Hemisphere itself. It is coming very close to home," he warned.[23]

No one questioned the legitimacy of an American military response if the nation was attacked. But just what was an attack in an age of modern warfare? The word "attack" had to be reinterpreted, Roosevelt argued. Some urged that the United States should not be considered under attack "until bombs actually drop in the streets of New York or San Francisco or New Orleans or Chicago. But they are simply shutting their eyes to the lesson that we must learn from the fate of every Nation that the Nazis have conquered." Any ambiguity in the country's deeper engagement with war would be wiped away, of course, when Japan attacked that December, but Roosevelt had opened the door to an argument that starting a war could be "defensive," an argument that would reappear in later years in the form of "preemptive" war against Iraq.[24]

Defense of the nation would require more than a military presence in the Atlantic, however. It required the dedication of Americans. "Your Government has the right to expect of all citizens that they take part in the common work of our common defense—take loyal part from this moment forward," Roosevelt insisted. This would involve "using every available resource; it means enlarging every useful plant," and it meant guarding against the influence of "fifth columnists—who are the incendiary bombs in this country of the moment." He ended with a quintessentially American call to arms—the closing words from the Declaration of Independence: "With a firm reliance on the protection of Divine Providence, we mutually pledge to each other our lives, our fortunes, and our sacred honor."[25]

Roosevelt followed this stirring speech with a proclamation that "an unlimited national emergency confronts this country, which requires that its military, naval, air, and civilian defenses be put on the basis of readiness to repel any and all acts or threats of aggression directed toward any part of the Western Hemisphere." The public reacted positively, with the president's already high approval ratings going from 73 to 76 percent. In the aftermath of the speech, and with Americans more strongly in favor of action short of direct military conflict to protect American interests, Roosevelt announced the establishment of a base in Iceland. The Germans were flying reconnaissance regularly over Iceland and Greenland, so establishing a foothold in the North Atlantic seemed imperative.[26]

By November 1941, tensions had also escalated in the Pacific, and American leaders expected a Japanese attack at any time. As Secretary of War Henry Stimson recalled, they faced a problem. "If you know that your enemy is going to strike you, it is not usually wise to wait until he gets the jump on you," and instead more advantageous to take the initiative. Nevertheless, there was both benefit and danger in "letting the Japanese fire the first shot." It would leave "no doubt in anyone's mind as to who were the aggressors," helping the administration gain public support. As relations with Japan continued to deteriorate, commanding officers in Hawaii and elsewhere in the Pacific were notified that "hostile action" might take place at any time. If hostilities could not be avoided, Roosevelt, like Stimson, hoped that Japan would start it. Yet, as the military prepared for imminent war, Stimson later noted, "they were surrounded, outside of their offices and almost throughout the country, by a spirit of isolationism and disbelief in danger which now seems incredible."[27]

Stimson's somewhat shocking reaction to the news of Pearl Harbor is therefore understandable. "When the news first came that Japan had attacked us," he wrote in his diary, "my first feeling was of relief that the indecision was over and that a crisis had come in a way which would unite all our people."[28]

Roosevelt opened a cabinet meeting in the Oval Office on the evening of December 7, 1941, by remarking that it was "the most serious meeting of the Cabinet that had taken place since 1861," as the Civil War broke out. It is one thing to anticipate war, and another to receive the news that the nation was caught off-guard in Hawaii, many had perished, and American ships went down. The next day, Roosevelt delivered his "infamy" speech before a joint session of Congress. The American people would always "remember the character of the onslaught against us," he proclaimed, calling on Congress for a declaration of war with Japan. Within a week, Germany and Italy had declared war on the United States, and the U.S. formally joined the war in Europe.[29]

Although Pearl Harbor remains the focus of American memory, Japan also attacked the Philippines, Malaya, Hong Kong, and Guam, on the same day. The first draft of Roosevelt's address highlighted the attacks on both Hawaii and the Philippines, but he removed all but one mention of the Philippines from his speech. Hawaii was a territory of the United States, one which would gain statehood not long after the war, and the Philippines a colony. Historian Emily Rosenberg argues that emphasizing Hawaii reflected "Roosevelt's fear that the damage might not be perceived as hitting close enough to home to crush isolationist sentiment." Rather than a blitz of many far-flung islands,

Roosevelt emphasized an attack on America. In doing so, he made Pearl Harbor the iconic event we remember today.[30]

In the aftermath, the nation's long, slow entry into World War II was quickly eclipsed by the shock of Pearl Harbor. Stimson later testified at a Pearl Harbor inquiry: "From some of the comments quoted in the public press, one would get the impression that the imminent threat of war in October and November 1941 was a deep secret, known only to the authorities in Washington who kept it mysteriously to themselves."[31] The president did not keep knowledge of the nation's lengthier involvement in World War II from the American people, but he did hope to avoid scrutiny of the fact that, long before war was declared, he was fully acting as commander in chief, amassing an army, deploying weaponry, supplying allies. And reinforcing the idea of the war's beginning at Pearl Harbor enabled a narrative of infamy, Rosenberg argues, "establishing American military action as reactive and defensive." James Reston reported in the *New York Times*: "By not the slightest indication did [President Roosevelt] suggest that the facts of the world situation had finally justified his policy, as even his opponents were admitting . . . he might very well have done." Pearl Harbor was "a political godsend for President Roosevelt," historian John Dower writes, and "the perception that, for all its horrors, December 7 was also a blessing did not come as delayed hindsight." It was a feature of the immediate news coverage. "Thanks now to Japan," declared the *Chicago Daily News*, "the deep division of opinion that has rent and paralyzed our country will be swiftly healed." What was shocking at the time of Pearl Harbor was Japan's unanticipated military effectiveness,

Redding, California, December 7, 1941: A young boy sells newspapers announcing the Japanese attack on Pearl Harbor. Photo by Anthony Potter Collection/Getty Images.

and the level of American vulnerability. It was not a shock at the time that the United States was at war.[32]

THE COURT AT WAR

There were important consequences of this final step in a longer path toward war. Within two weeks of Pearl Harbor, Congress passed a war powers act, which authorized the president to "reorganize the federal government virtually as he saw fit," as the constitutional historian Paul Murphy described it. Other measures followed, and Roosevelt made clear that he would forge ahead with or without Congress. In seeking repeal of a provision of the Price Control Act in September 1942, he warned that if Congress did not cooperate, "it will leave me with an inescapable responsibility to the people of this country to see that the war effort is no longer imperiled by economic chaos." And on February 19, 1942, in a vast incursion on civil liberties, the president ordered the removal from the West Coast and internment in camps of Japanese American citizens and Japanese immigrants, depriving them of any means of demonstrating that their imprisonment served no military purpose.[33]

Justices of the Supreme Court had joined Congress for Roosevelt's December 8 address. The solemn event moved Hugo Black to tears. Even Felix Frankfurter, who carefully followed war news and was deeply troubled by the dangers facing European Jews, thought of December 7 as a watershed. "Everything has changed," he told his law clerk, "and I am going to war." Frankfurter would become, in Paul Murphy's words, "the most advanced war hawk on the Court."[34]

The newest Justice, Robert Jackson, who had so recently been attorney general and was confirmed to the Court during the summer of 1941, now regretted his more sequestered role. After Pearl Harbor, he told the president that he "felt I was in sort of a back eddy. I was not doing anything that promoted the war effort and not much that seemed to be very important in contrast with the great issues at stake in the world." Jackson offered to leave the Court, but Roosevelt insisted that he remain. Justice James Byrnes resigned to head the Office of Economic Stabilization and then to serve as director of the Office of War Mobilization. Frank Murphy remained on the Court, but sought a more active war-related role. To the consternation of his colleagues, Murphy accepted a commission as a lieutenant colonel in the army. He would be on duty but in an inactive status during Court recesses, so that he would not have to resign his Court seat.[35]

Even though December 7 and the declaration of war were catalytic events, the Court, like the president and Congress, had been involved in war work well before Pearl Harbor. Issues involving national security, fueled by international affairs, did not wait for war to be declared before spilling over into other areas of life. Just as "wartime" could not contain war powers, neither could it contain incursions on civil liberties.

In 1936 Roosevelt summoned J. Edgar Hoover to the White House. The situation in Europe had heightened concerns about national security and domestic subversion. Congress joined the fray, first establishing the Dies Committee on un-American activities in the House in May 1938, and passing the Hatch Act, which embodied, as Paul Murphy has written, "the first anti-Communist prohibition in federal employment" in August 1939. These developments were part of a domestic "security drama" from 1938 to 1947, that was in part a standoff between Congress and the White House, as security was politicized. Domestic security concerns during the late 1930s were small compared to what was happening internationally, but the crisis that culminated during the World War II years had already begun to play out, on the home front as well as in the military theater, in the late 1930s.[36]

For many Americans, the rise of fascism in Europe made American liberties seem more precious. The Democratic Party's 1940 plank urged support for civil liberties, in light of the "vivid contrast between the freedom we enjoy and the dark repression which prevails in the lands where liberty is dead." The German experience did more than demonstrate the importance of rights, however. It illustrated a weakness of majoritarian government. In the absence of political restraints, an inflamed populace could sweep a dictator into power, creating the conditions for undermining their own freedom. The rise of fascism around the world, coupled with deprivation and unrest at home, also led to anxiety over the future of democratic government itself. In this context, some American intellectuals placed their hope in the judicial branch. Walter Lippman thought that an independent judiciary was the "vital center" of constitutional democracy and a source of protection against the abuses of a "transient and hysterical majority." The idea that American courts were a safeguard against fascism brought the international crisis into the domestic political storm brewing over the Supreme Court.[37]

In 1937, when Roosevelt announced a plan to pack the Court, to reduce the influence of conservative justices who had struck down New Deal programs, many raised questions about its impact on the constitutional balance of powers. The most common critique was that it made Roosevelt too powerful, reminiscent of the dictators in other nations. The journalist Dorothy Thompson, testifying in a congressional hearing, argued that "if any President wanted to establish a dictatorship and do so with all the appearance of legality, this is the way he would take." But the court-packing plan also generated "more elaborate and sophisticated criticisms," notes the legal writer David Bixby. Because it undermined judicial independence from the executive branch, the plan stood to weaken the branch that most protected the United States from fascism. For Lippman, as Bixby put it, "the growth of fascism in Europe . . . demonstrated how groups could exploit the rights of free speech and assembly in order to obtain a mandate from the majority to discard democracy and establish a totalitarian regime." Similarly, Thompson argued that "the prevention against today's majority mortgaging tomorrow's majority, lay in a written constitution and an independent Supreme Court to interpret that Constitution." These concerns were reinforced when German and Italian newspapers came out in support of the plan. It generated "excited banner headlines" in Berlin, the *Washington Post* reported. And the Italian press cheered Roosevelt "as a champion of vigorous leadership against 'outworn' methods of government."[38] The specter of fascism in Europe was, for some Americans, reason enough to protect the Court's autonomy and reject the court-packing plan.

During the late 1930s, heightened concern over national security led states to pass new laws punishing sedition and requiring loyalty oaths. The Supreme Court pushed back, however, overturning the conviction of Dirk De Jonge for criminal syndicalism, for helping to organize a Communist Party meeting in Oregon, finding his activities protected under the First Amendment. The Court also overturned Angelo Herndon's conviction for inciting insurrection by encouraging African Americans to join the Communist Party in Georgia.[39]

The Court's solicitude toward civil liberties would have its limits, however. One of the more dramatic battles over rights during the World War II era began to play out well before Pearl Harbor. The controversy involved schoolchildren who were Jehovah's Witnesses and who refused to salute the American flag. Under the students' religious beliefs, saluting the flag was the equivalent of worshipping a graven image, which was sinful. States passed laws requiring the flag salute in public schools, and students who refused could be expelled. The controversy was just one of many ways the Witnesses came into conflict with local governments, as their devoted efforts at proselytizing led to prosecution. Viewing the Witnesses as un-American, mobs beat them, ransacked their homes, and terrorized these communities repeatedly during the late 1930s and the 1940s.[40]

In the first cases involving the Witnesses, the Supreme Court ruled in their favor. In the late 1930s, the Court struck down, on First Amendment grounds, city ordinances prohibiting the distribution of religious literature, and restricting door-to-door distribution. In *Minersville School District v. Gobitis* (1940), however, the Court upheld the constitutionality of a flag-salute law. Lillian and William Gobitas [*sic*], Jehovah's Witnesses, ages twelve and ten, who had refused to salute the flag, were expelled from public school.[41]

Walter Gobitas and his children, William and Lillian, leaving the federal courthouse in Philadelphia, Pennsylvania, February 16, 1938. Bettmann/CORBIS.

Gobitis was argued in the Supreme Court on April 25, 1940. By then, Germany had overrun Poland, Norway, and Denmark. Hitler launched an offensive against Belgium, the Netherlands, and Luxembourg on May 10, and then turned on France. The Court decided *Gobitis* on June 3, eleven days before the Germans marched into Paris. France surrendered on June 25. The American public was consumed with this news. Justice Frankfurter was preoccupied by the war. "Hardly anything else" had been on his mind, he wrote Roosevelt in late May. He himself tied the international crisis to his work on the *Gobitis* opinion and, the law and religion scholar Shawn Francis Peters writes, he "privately touted the notion that the Supreme Court had an obligation to consider the critical importance of national

security when it weighed the constitutional issues at stake."
The "time and circumstances are surely not irrelevant considerations in resolving the conflicts," Frankfurter wrote to
Justice Harlan Fiske Stone, who would be the lone dissenter.
The wartime context mattered to finding the right balance
between "legislatively allowable pursuit of national security and the right to stand on individual idiosyncracies."[42]

Writing the majority opinion upholding the flag-salute
law in *Gobitis*, Frankfurter emphasized that "we are dealing
with an interest inferior to none in the hierarchy of legal
values. National unity is the basis of national security." The
Justice did not leave the context of war to the imagination,
invoking one of Lincoln's famous statements. "Situations
like the present are phases of the profoundest problem con-
fronting a democracy," Frankfurter wrote, "the problem
which Lincoln cast in memorable dilemma. 'Must a government of necessity be too strong for the liberties of its
people, or too weak to maintain its own existence?'" Lincoln
was facing the secession of southern states. In comparison,
a flag salute requirement might seem a less weighty government imperative. But for Frankfurter, "the ultimate foundation of a free society is the binding tie of cohesive
sentiment." "We live," he wrote, "by symbols." The flag was
the symbol of national unity, "transcending all internal differences, however large, within the framework of the Constitution." And that grey spring, when Hitler marched
through Europe, Frankfurter felt both the importance of
national solidarity, and also a need for courts to leave
weighty questions like these to the political branches. The
"subtle process of securing effective loyalty to the traditional ideals of democracy," was not the province of the
courts, Frankfurter wrote. The Court's 8–1 ruling upheld

the Minersville law, and, perceived as legitimating anti-Witness sentiment, unleashed an unprecedented wave of violence against them. Some Supreme Court law clerks, critical of the outcome, referred to *Gobitis* as "Felix's Fall of France Opinion."[43]

The constitutional controversy over the Witnesses was far from over, however. Their cause would be aided by changes on the Court. In 1941 Justice Jackson took the seat of Justice Stone, who was elevated to Chief Justice when Charles Evans Hughes retired. Justice James Byrnes left the Court for war work in the fall of 1942, and was replaced by the staunch civil libertarian Wiley B. Rutledge.[44]

In 1942, when a slim majority upheld municipal license fees as applied to Witnesses selling literature door-to-door, three members of the *Gobitis* majority—Justices Hugo Black, William O. Douglas, and Frank Murphy—used the occasion to express regret for *Gobitis* in a dissenting opinion. Then, a year later, the Court overturned *Gobitis*, and struck down a West Virginia flag-salute law in *West Virginia State Board of Education v. Barnette* (1943), finding that a compulsory flag-salute law violated the First Amendment. The Court did not abandon Frankfurter's concern about national security. Instead, the majority had a different view about how national security is best protected. Justice Jackson, writing for the majority, took up Frankfurter's invocation of Lincoln, but wrote that "it may be doubted whether Mr. Lincoln would have thought that the strength of government to maintain itself would be impressively vindicated by our confirming power of the state to expel a handful of children from school."[45]

At the heart of the case, however, was the question of whether the compulsory flag-salute requirement was an appropriate way to safeguard national security. "Struggles to coerce uniformity of sentiment in support of some end thought essential to their time and country have been waged by many good as well as by evil men," Jackson wrote. When "moderate methods to attain unity have failed, those bent on its accomplishment must resort to an ever-increasing severity." Yet efforts to compel national unity could only fail, Jackson argued, and this was "the lesson of every such effort from the Roman drive to stamp out Christianity as a disturber of its pagan unity, . . . down to the fast failing efforts of our present totalitarian enemies." Ultimately, "those who begin coercive elimination of dissent soon find themselves exterminating dissenters. Compulsory unification of opinion achieves only the unanimity of the graveyard."[46] National security was ultimately hampered, not enhanced, by punishing dissenters.

The antitotalitarian rhetoric of Jackson's opinion, and the date of the case itself, falling within the dates of a declared war, leads scholars to cite *Barnette* as an example of the way rights can actually expand in wartime. *Gobitis* is sometimes thought of as a peacetime case, so that the context of wartime is new in *Barnette*, and wartime helps determine the outcome.[47] But on closer analysis, what drives the different outcomes in the flag-salute cases is not the difference between wartime and peacetime, for the context of war weighed on the justices as they decided both *Gobitis* and *Barnette*. Instead the cases represent different ideas of how to safeguard national security in a dangerous world.

Throughout the 1930s, 1940s, and 1950s, judges, legislators, litigants, and others often conceptualized rights in terms of national security.[48] Rights could expand or contract in ways that aided war-related governance or enhanced national security. The example of the flag-salute cases signals a broader problem: When we assume that security is at issue only in temporally confined wartimes, we miss the more pervasive influence of military conflict on American law.

Japanese officials signed surrender documents on September 2, 1945, bringing a formal end to hostilities between two nations.[49] But the power of war could not quite be extinguished with a signature. The United States began to demobilize, but the draft would persist, and a legal state of war, enabling the use of government war powers, would endure for several years.

World War II would maintain a hold on the imagination of Americans. It was the "good war," remembered as a moment of national unity and purpose. As the journalist Tom Brokaw described the World War II generation: "They answered the call to help save the world. . . . They faced great odds . . . but they did not protest." World War II is thought to be a good war mainly because its cause was just, but it is also remembered as a traditional American war because it was formally declared by Congress, and it is perceived as having a clear beginning and ending. The frustrations of the war in Vietnam—with its controversial and gradual escalation—would only elevate World War II as an example of the right way to fight a war. It would be memorialized in film, fiction, and memoir as a real and honorable war.[50]

World War II became for Americans what war should be. It reinforced the idea that real wars were large-scale conflicts with other powerful nations, punctuated by peacetimes. This conception of the "American way of war" limits our thinking, the military analyst Jeffrey Record argues. It keeps us focused on large-scale wars, to the exclusion of more common, smaller-scale wars, and this undermines the strategic effectiveness of the U.S. military by focusing training on outdated models.

This framing of war also affects law and politics, reinforcing our belief that real wars are big conflicts, bound in time. The focus on iconic wars of the past keeps us from understanding the impact on American law and politics of the kind of war we now experience. Constitutional law, for example, continues to be bound up in an imagined World War II model, so that, as chapter 1 illustrates, leading scholars believe that a war between nation-states, bound in time, is what a war is.[51]

Even World War II was fuzzier around the edges than we usually imagine. In the years that followed, as postwar became Cold War, a different model of warfare competed for attention, only to be collapsed into the memory of wars past. But that is a story for the next chapter.

3

What Kind of War Was the Cold War?

MAJOR ARTHUR D. NICHOLSON IS thought of as the last American Cold War casualty. The circumstances of his death, and the way it is remembered, are fraught with ambiguity. Nicholson was in East Germany, on the other side of the Iron Curtain, on March 24, 1985, on an intelligence gathering mission. While photographing a Soviet storage facility, he was shot by a Soviet sentry.[1]

Nicholson was a member of the United States Military Liaison Mission, a fourteen-member unit charged with observing Soviet activities in East Germany. The unit was created in 1947 following the Potsdam conference to act as a liaison between American and Soviet zones of occupation in Germany. Under this arrangement, American soldiers could enter Soviet-occupied East Germany and conduct a form of sanctioned spying on Soviet installations. Some areas were off-limits.[2]

The mission was dangerous. To see anything worth observing, the American units had to avoid the Soviet secret police, which would tail them and engage in high-speed chases, sometimes in the dark without lights. Six times prior to Nicholson's death, Soviet gunfire had hit U.S. Military Liaison vehicles. The Soviets sometimes crashed large military trucks into the smaller American vehicles. In 1984 a French officer was killed in a crash as the Soviets tried to hamper reconnaissance by "offensively disturbing" vehicles.[3]

Nicholson and a driver were gathering intelligence near the town of Ludwigslust. The Soviets later claimed that he was in an unauthorized area, and "penetrated directly into the territory of that installation and photographed combat equipment and was caught red-handed by a Soviet sentry." This was a "flagrant violation" of the 1947 agreement, the Soviets argued. The sentry only fired after Nicholson ignored repeated warnings to halt, and after a warning shot was fired, the Soviets insisted. Nicholson's death was a "tragic outcome," but the responsibility lay with the United States. American officials objected that this "murder" was unjustified and that following the shooting, Nicholson lay wounded "for a considerable time without medical attention while his driver was forced to remain in his car." To President Ronald Reagan, Nicholson's "cold-blooded murder" was a reflection of "the difference between the two societies: one that has no regard for human life, and one like our own that thinks it's the most important thing."[4]

The shooting happened at a pivotal moment. Just two weeks earlier, Mikhail Gorbachev had assumed power in the Soviet Union. This may have tempered the American response, as Reagan, in spite of his statement, hoped that the shooting would not undermine the possibility of a summit with the new leader. In addition, the Americans and the Soviets were negotiating at that time in Geneva regarding the use of space weapons, including Reagan's "Star Wars" space antimissile defense system. Tamping down on the rhetoric, a State Department spokesperson said: "'We're trying to avoid turning this into another K.A.L. affair,' referring to the shooting down of a South Korean airliner, with 269 people aboard, by a Soviet fighter plane in 1983," which Reagan had also denounced, and which fueled Cold War tensions.[5]

As diplomatic wrangling continued, the American public reacted to Nicholson's killing. Nearly 350 people in Atlantic Highlands, New Jersey, bared their backsides in the direction of the Soviet Union as a sign of contempt. When Nicholson's body was returned to the United States, Vice President George H. W. Bush described him as "an outstanding officer murdered in the line of duty."[6]

Was Nicholson murdered? Was he a victim, as is written on a commemorative plaque placed at the site of the killing in East Germany?[7] Or was he a soldier killed in battle—albeit a long, slow battle we call the Cold War?

Nicholson was laid to rest in Arlington National Cemetery, beneath a headstone that reads: "Killed in East Germany, U.S. Military Liaison Mission." The Veterans of Foreign Wars object to this form of ambiguous remembrance. "No mention is made of who killed him or why he was shot," argued an editorial in the *VFW Magazine*. "This is reflective of how many Americans who preceded Nicholson in death during the Cold War are remembered."[8]

Arthur Nicholson's body came to rest in a shifting terrain. Even as he bled to death in a field in East Germany, the historical category of his military service—the Cold War—was beginning to collapse. The nature of this death and its consequences depended on whether it fit into a period that we call wartime. But if this soldier died in battle, it was not the sort of battle imagined by Clausewitz.[9] Nicholson's weapon was a camera. He had no accompanying battalion. He was a liminal figure in an ambiguous era, and his death seemed to trigger a need to stabilize the categories.

THE COLD WAR AND THE
IDEA OF WARTIME

The Cold War era was a time of anxiety in America, and nothing captured this more clearly than the image of a clock. The Doomsday Clock, which measured movement toward a nuclear apocalypse, was first called "The Clock of Doom" when it appeared in June 1947. It was meant to represent the concerns of nuclear scientists, but soon became a ubiquitous symbol of nuclear danger. In 1953, after both the United States and the Soviet Union tested powerful thermonuclear bombs, the hands of the clock moved to two minutes to midnight, so that, in the words of Eugene Rabinowitch, editor of the *Bulletin of Atomic Scientists*, "only a few more swings of the pendulum, . . . and atomic explosions will strike midnight for Western civilization." Although the hands of the clock symbolized impending doom, they moved only fourteen times in forty-eight years, sometimes forward and sometimes backward, and never more than seven minutes at a time.[10] In that sense the clock was largely a representation of time standing still. Across the years, the world remained tethered to the same moment, a moment of impending nuclear annihilation.

George Orwell wrote in the fall of 1945 that the bomb was likely to change the structure of global politics. Weak states would become weaker, and "two or three monstrous super-states," each with nuclear weapons, would "divid[e] the world between them." These monster states would not use the bomb against each other. Instead, they would be "unconquerable and in a permanent state of 'cold war'" with their neighbors. The nuclear age would therefore bring "an

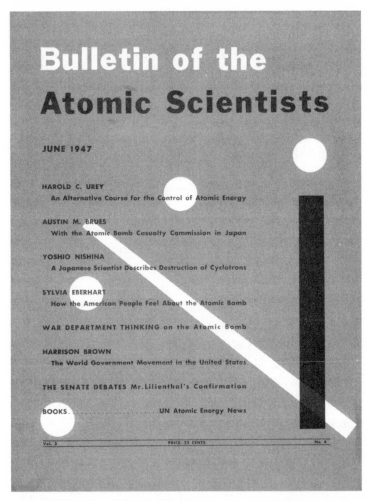

The "Doomsday Clock" first appeared on the cover of the *Bulletin of the Atomic Scientists* in June 1947. It became a widely recognized symbol of nuclear anxiety. Martyl Langsdorf, *Bulletin of the Atomic Scientists* (June 1947), cover. Copyright © 1947 by Bulletin of the Atomic Scientists, Chicago, Illinois. Reproduced with permission.

end to large-scale wars at the cost of prolonging indefinitely 'a peace that is no peace.'"[11]

The idea of a cold war was, of course, intentionally contradictory. The term was popularized by Walter Lippman and Bernard Baruch, and had entered American political discourse by 1947. But the question of what it was, and even when it happened, have ever since been subjects of debate. Whether the Cold War was wartime, peacetime, some sort of hybrid, or simply a historical time-marker is a question of more than historical interest. After 9/11, scholars searching for historical comparisons argued that the new security-infused environment shared characteristics with the Cold War, with frightening implications for contemporary policymaking.[12]

The Cold War is regularly invoked by contemporary writers focusing on war and social change, but without examining definitional ambiguities. If there are to be lessons from the Cold War era for our own day, it is important to focus on just what it was, and how it fits in the history of American wartimes.

During the Cold War there were no cataclysmic battles and great victories, but small wars, surveillance, and stalemate. As we've seen, however, the understanding of war that has dominated American military planning as well as legal and political thought is that of large-scale military engagements with other powerful nations, punctuated by peacetimes. Even though the Cold War was an era of limited, smaller-scale wars, military planners retained their focus on large-scale wars. Scholars of law and politics also retained this framing, so that the study of war's impact on American life has focused on the iconic wars of the past, leaving out the limited wars that have become dominant.[13]

The Cold War's ambiguity might have signaled that the conventional categories no longer fit—that wartime and peacetime coexisted or had merged together. Arguments along these lines informed policymakers during the late 1940s and early 1950s, and were part of the discourse of national security state building. But rather than viewing the Cold War years as dismantling conventional categories of war and peace, contemporary thinkers find ways to fit that era into preexisting conceptual boxes. For some writers, the Cold War becomes an old-fashioned "wartime."[14]

Nuclear weapons ushered in the Cold War, but actual nuclear war would have meant widespread global destruction. Many writers in the late 1940s and the 1950s described the Cold War as anything short of World War III. If the Cold War was anything short of World War III, and if World War III meant global annihilation, the Cold War was anything short of an apocalypse. In this rendering, the Cold War was defined in reference to an imaginary. Underlying Cold War–era anxiety was the idea that once nuclear weapons were created, nuclear conflagration was inevitable.[15]

This idea is captured in the 1959 film *On the Beach*. In the film, clouds of deadly radiation from nuclear war drifted slowly and inevitably to Australia, home to the world's final living inhabitants. The war itself seemed the result of inevitable human folly once nuclear weapons came into existence. It was left to the Australians and a band of American submariners to await their terrible fate, armed only with suicide pills. A final image of the town square carried a contradictory message. "There is Still Time!" blared the banner of a religious group, yet the square's windblown emptiness belied the message.[16]

The anxieties of the nuclear age were manifested in national security politics. As the historian Michael J. Hogan argues, Cold War struggles over American policy and the nature of the state were about more than combating communism. Also at stake was American national identity, the nation's role in the world, and the impact of Cold War policies on domestic institutions.[17]

After World War II, Americans hoped for a return to peacetime concerns. Leaders worked to restructure political control of the military, but were divided in their perceptions of international conditions. "The central challenge of state-making in the early Cold War," Hogan argues, "was to prepare for permanent struggle without surrendering constitutional principles and democratic traditions to the garrison state." In battles over the budget and military policy, some policymakers viewed the idea of distinctions between war and peace to be a "technicality" outmoded in a new era "when the United States had to be prepared for war on a permanent basis." In framing American national security policy, Secretary of State Dean Acheson and others argued that the Cold War was "in fact a real war," against a nation that was determined to achieve "world domination." President Harry S. Truman initially pushed back, trying to maintain the idea of a peacetime world, and insisting that his policies were not "mobilization for war," but instead "preparedness." But Truman himself encouraged war fever to generate support for the foreign aid directives outlined in his "Truman Doctrine" speech in 1947. By the early 1950s, with the onset of the Korean War, Truman's effort to maintain the categories of war and peace, and to shift policy to peacetime pursuits, collapsed in the face of efforts to cast the Cold War "as a permanent struggle of global proportions." As conditions worsened in Korea, political battles over the balance between national security and domestic priorities like a balanced budget were resolved in favor of security, and, as Hogan argues, "national security concerns became the common currency of most policy makers, the arbiter of most values, the key to America's new identity." In American national security ideology, "the distinction between war and peace had disappeared," as the government transitioned from a New Deal state to a national security state.[18]

A national security state with an ongoing focus on military engagement needed both a new bureaucratic structure and a new language of government. The National Security Act of 1947 brought American military branches under one bureaucratic umbrella. The Department of War became the Department of Defense, and there would be a secretary of defense instead of a secretary of war. Military budgets were not war spending but defense spending. Even as the first major hot war of the Cold War began in Korea, American leaders were framing military action continents away as a means of defending the American way of life. American soldiers fought in Korea, but they were seen as defending their own nation against a broader and more amorphous threat: communism.[19]

If the United States had entered a new era, one in which war and not-war coexisted, this was in tension with the traditional separation of war and peace, and yet these distinctions remained resilient. "Americans are wont to regard war and peace as sharply distinctive conditions," writes the British military strategist Colin S. Gray. The notion that wartime is exceptional is a part of American military culture. "Americans have approached warfare as a regrettable occasional evil that has to be concluded as decisively and rapidly as possible," and soldiers "have always been prepared nearly exclusively for 'real war,' which is to say combat against a tolerably symmetrical, regular enemy."[20] Yet during and after the Cold War, American military conflict defied these conceptual categories.

WAS THE COLD WAR A WAR?

Americans during the 1940s and 1950s knew they were in a "cold war," but as the historian Kenneth Osgood notes, many did not quite know what it was, and were unable to define it. In a 1955 poll, some responded that it was "'war through talking,' . . . 'war without actual fighting,' 'political war,'" while others thought of it as "just like a hot war," or "real war all over the world." Osgood writes that most Americans "perceived the Cold War as a war, but as a different kind of war—one that was difficult to define, one that was fought not so much with guns and tanks and atom bombs, as with words and ideas and political maneuvers all over the world."[21]

So just what was it? "Cold War," notes the historian Odd Arne Westad, along with "Third World" was "a late-twentieth century neo-logism" which was "employed for various purposes and in various settings to create some of the most hegemonic discourses of the era." By the 1950s, he writes, the term Cold War "came to signal an American concept of warfare against the Soviet Union: aggressive containment without a state of war." After the collapse of the Soviet Union, in Russia and in the West, in popular parlance "the Cold War has come to be seen simply as a conflict of national interests—two giant countries faced each other and battled it out for world supremacy by most means short of all-out war, or until one of them was too exhausted to fight any longer." But the idea that the Cold War was a period defined by fighting that stopped short of direct war is misleading, for as the historian Lori Lynn Bogle puts it, this "does not explain the warfare that did occur along the peripheries." Cold War–era warfare included major wars in Korea and Vietnam, but also smaller-scale military engagements in Asia, Africa, Latin America, and the Middle East. For the historian Anders Stephanson, the Cold War's meaning hovers between war and warlike. Battles between its key antagonists did not take place "in the two-dimensional space of traditional battles" but elsewhere. "Real war, meanwhile, is displaced beyond the militarized heartlands onto the 'periphery' articulated in regional and local conflict."[22]

How is such an ambiguous phenomenon represented in works of U.S. history? The Cold War most often functions as simply a time-period—a way to break up segments of the past into manageable units, so that a history text will have a World War II chapter, followed by a Cold War chapter. But periodization depends on the Cold War's definition, and so is itself contested. Most scholars put this era's starting point somewhere between 1945 and 1947, and it is commonly thought to have ended between 1989 and 1991 with the thawing of U.S.-Soviet relations, the fall of the Berlin Wall, and the ultimate dissolution of the Soviet Union. Scholars of Asia and Africa see it differently. David Anderson argues that the Cold War in Africa came to a close with the Rwandan genocide in 1994. Writing about Asia, Christopher Bailey and Tim Harper argue that even World War II was merely a phase of a longer period of conflict from the 1937 Japanese attack on China to the 1980s. For Eric Hobsbawm, the Cold War is part of an "Age of Extremes" that spanned "the Short Twentieth Century" from 1914 to the early 1990s when this "era in world history ended and a new one began."[23]

The ambiguities of the Cold War that plague scholars drop away for soldiers deployed during its military engagements. Veterans' organizations have argued that the Cold War warrants a military campaign service medal, just like other American wartimes. Soldiers receive medals not just for major wars like World War II, but also for service in smaller wars like Lebanon (1959) and Grenada (1983). The time span for the proposed Cold War medal eligibility would be from September 2, 1945, through December 26, 1991, following a periodization close to that used by most diplomatic historians who do not track direct military engagement but instead a particular era of U.S.-Soviet relations.[24] Because of this, the Cold War medal proposal essentially turns a diplomatic era into an old-fashioned wartime.

As Major Nicholson's story shows, there is controversy over how to remember the Cold War, and this seems to have stymied efforts to create a medal for it. Senators Susan M. Collins and Blanche L. Lincoln, former Senator Hillary Rodham Clinton, and others cosponsored Cold War medal legislation in 2007 and earlier years. Congress created an honorary certificate for both soldiers and civilians, but medal legislation has not been enacted. Opposition stems from the cost, although cost has not impeded awarding service medals to veterans of countless lesser-known conflicts.[25] Due to the stalemate, Congress seems

Proposed Cold War Medal. Photograph by Maria Iacabo. Medal courtesy of Charles P. McDowell, Foxfall Medals, Madison, Virginia.

to remain on the fence on the question of whether the Cold War was a "war."

For veterans' organizations that base membership on wartime service, there is no ambiguity. The years following World War II are seen as times of war. The Veterans of Foreign Wars, for example, honors service in Cuba, 1961; Thailand, 1962; Vietnam, 1965–1973; Iran, Yemen, and the Indian Ocean, 1978–1981; and 30 consecutive days of service in Korea at any time. From 1945 on, even excluding Berlin (1945–1990), American service members have been deployed somewhere in the world under conditions that enable eligibility. For the Veterans of Foreign Wars, war has been ongoing since World War II.[26]

Military service medals and VFW membership are based on service in the face of hostile fire. Diplomatic historians, by and large, frame the contours of the Cold War by reference to U.S.-Soviet diplomatic relations, and not according to the traditional markers of warfare, such as when the first attack and counterattack occurred. This all may seem obvious, but these details drop away when we turn to the way the Cold War figures in the history of American civil liberties. Writers seem to assume that they are building on a description of geopolitics established by historians of war and diplomacy, yet the international context is more often assumed than engaged, so that for scholars of domestic law and politics, sometimes the Cold War is treated as if it functioned like an old-fashioned war.

THE COLD WAR AND SOCIAL CHANGE

Historians often write about war as if it were an agent of change, doing things beyond any battlefield. "World War II shattered a world irrevocably," the historian Manning Marable writes. For Alan Brinkley, although the fighting was remote from most Americans, the war "profoundly . . . changed America." The Cold War is also referred to as a historical actor. "It would be impossible to list the ways the Cold War changed our lives," writes the military historian Robert Cowley.[27]

The historical dimensions of the Cold War at home are familiar. The years after World War II were a low point for American civil liberties. Anticommunism fueled American politics, and labor leaders, entertainment figures, civil rights activists, and others were hounded by antisubversive boards, blacklisted out of employment, and sometimes imprisoned. Anticommunist scapegoating during the late 1940s and the 1950s is unquestioned, but its relationship to the geopolitical conflict is not always clear. "The Cold War was crucial" to the anticommunist repression of the late 1940s and 1950s, writes Ellen Schrecker, a leading scholar of anticommunism, "though exactly how it contributed to the growth of McCarthyism is not as self-evident as it may superficially appear."[28]

The timing of this era of American repression doesn't completely coincide with the broader Cold War conflict between the United States and the Soviet Union. The Cold War lasted until at least 1989, but the red-baiting of this era was on the wane by the late 1950s, and was largely eclipsed in the mid-1960s when, prodded in part by the civil rights movement, courts and legislatures expanded civil rights, free speech rights, the rights of criminal defendants, reproductive rights, and more. When writers argue that the Cold War drove the deprivation of rights, it can appear as though the times themselves are determining the action, as when Bertrand Barère during the French Revolution claimed that his era compelled his acts of repression. He did not shape his epoch, he said, but only "did what I had to do, obey it."[29] If post–World War II red-baiting was driven by the Cold War, how could the periodization of the Cold War and the red scare be so different? If Cold War repression was a form of "wartime" repression, after all, the repression would be expected to linger to the war's end.

We can examine this problem more closely through a prominent example of the impact of the crusade against communism on individual rights: the prosecution of Communist Party members under the Smith Act, which criminalized advocating the violent overthrow of the United States. The Smith Act itself was not a product of the Cold War; it was passed in 1940. The most significant Smith Act prosecutions began in the late 1940s, during the Cold War. Even before the Soviet Union had tested their own nuclear bomb, the Truman administration was concerned that Americans were passing atomic secrets to its enemy. Due to ties with the Soviet Union, the American Communist Party came under particular scrutiny. Attorney General Tom C. Clark secured an indictment of party leaders for conspiracy, and eleven were convicted following a contentious trial. Others went underground to escape arrest.[30]

There were bona fide espionage cases during the Cold War, including prosecutions for passing nuclear secrets to the Soviets, but the Smith Act case turned on no such evidence. The defendants were charged instead with advocating radical change, not with acting on their beliefs. The evidence against them did not consist of testimony of acts of sabotage, but of works by Karl Marx, Frederick Engels, and other communist writers that party members read and discussed. The Supreme Court upheld the convictions in *United States v. Dennis* (1950). Justice Felix Frankfurter argued in a concurrence that the dangers of communism were so clear that the Court could take judicial notice of them. For the dissenting Justice William O. Douglas, however, the defendants' ideas could best be challenged by political argument, not imprisonment. He acknowledged dangers from Soviet aggression, but in the United States communism had failed as a political movement. Members of the American Communist Party were "miserable merchants of unwanted ideas; their wares remain unsold. The fact that their ideas are abhorrent does not make them powerful."[31]

Many view the era of the Smith Act prosecutions as an example of the way law failed during the Cold War era. In spite of constitutional protection of speech, freedom of association, and more, people were prosecuted not for plotting to overthrow the government, but for thinking, reading, and talking about revolution. The prosecutions were a major reason behind the decline of the American Communist Party, the legal historian Michal Belknap argues, and the nation as a whole "paid a high price for the debilitation of a small radical organization, for the methods used to incapacitate it seriously endangered rights lying at the heart of the American constitutional system." But this and other examples of anticommunist repression did not last for the duration of the Cold War itself. Instead, the public lost its tolerance of government overreaching, such as the reliance on tainted testimony, and the Supreme Court, now led by the legendary Chief Justice Earl Warren, narrowed the reach of the Smith Act in 1957. In *Yates v. United States* and other cases, the Court made Smith Act prosecutions more difficult, narrowing the scope of illegal acts to advocacy of concrete action to overthrow the government, rather than advocacy of abstract Communist doctrine. The Court would shift further toward protecting rights within a few years, striking down as unconstitutional a requirement that Communist Party members could not apply for passports in *Aptheker v. Secretary of State* in 1964. By this time, the Court's shift in a more progressive direction was solidified by the retirement of Justices Frankfurter and Charles E. Whittaker in 1962, and their replacement with the generally rights-friendly Justices Byron White and Arthur Goldberg. Similarly, Schrecker notes, while anticommunism has a longer history in twentieth-century America, it reached its zenith from 1946 to 1956.[32]

If the Cold War produced the red scare, just how did it do that, and why did red-baiting end before the Cold War was over? The leading First Amendment scholar Thomas Emerson, writing during the Cold War era, suggested that war can drive repression of free speech in a way similar to Eric J. Leed's description of the World War I trenches: chaos and fear abound, and time is suspended. "Emotions run high," Emerson wrote, "lowering the degree of rationality which is required to make such a system viable. . . . Immediate events assume greater importance; long-range considerations are pushed to the background." In this environment, "the need for consensus appears more urgent in the context of dealing with hostile outsiders. Cleavage seems to be more dangerous, and dissent more difficult to distinguish from actual aid to the enemy."[33]

Leading legal scholars see the Cold War as this kind of wartime. It is commonplace to argue, as Geoffrey Stone puts it, that because of the Cold War, the First Amendment was "in extremis." But how did a dispersed and often unconnected series of skirmishes add up to a wartime? "The Berlin blockade, the fall of China, and the Korean War were not independent events," Stone writes, "but part of a 'slow-motion hot war, conducted on the periphery of rival empires.'"[34]

Legal scholars tend to end their analysis of the Cold War's impact in the late 1950s, but a longer view illustrates that changes in individual rights don't neatly track the moments when global tensions rose and fell. For example, the Cuban Missile Crisis in October of 1962 was when the world came closest to nuclear war, but in 1962, free-speech restriction was not at its height. That year the Supreme Court decided landmark civil liberties cases, holding that states could not require prayer in public schools, and finding that the Court was not barred from considering a state's skewed voting districts, paving the way toward the requirement of one-person, one-vote. Meanwhile, the Kennedy administration supported James Meredith's efforts to enroll at the University of Mississippi, which had denied him admission because of his race.[35] Rights were expanding just as the nation came closest to nuclear war.

If repression of political rights during the late 1940s and 1950s was caused by the Cold War, why did the domestic scene change when it did? Some scholars argue, explicitly or implicitly, that the domestic Cold War ended in the late 1950s, when the impact on rights is less measurable. But this argument is circular. If international tension (the Cold War) is having an impact on rights at home, an easing of repression would need to come from geopolitical change, and the late fifties did not see a drop-off in Cold War tensions. The legal scholars Eric Posner and Adrian Vermeule have a different explanation for why this might have happened. They argue that crises, including wars, "have a half-life, and will decay over time." The reaction to the crisis will recede both because emotional reactions will abate and because "the government will downgrade its threat assessment, and judges will worry less and less about the harms from blocking emergency measures."[36]

Perhaps the disconnect between rights and geopolitics signals something more fundamental: that the rights restrictions during this era were driven more by domestic, than by geopolitical, developments in the first place. Thomas Emerson seemed to concur with this idea.

Although he believed that war was central to the history of civil liberties, when it came to the Cold War era, he did not see wartime as the driving issue. Instead, free speech violations during the McCarthy era and the Korean War years "did not relate directly to the war itself, but rather to a more general fear of communism within the United States." Stephen Feldman also emphasizes domestic factors in *Free Expression and Democracy in America: A History*. For Feldman, the origins of the Red Scare were in worsening relations between the United States and the Soviet Union, but this was drawn on in electoral politics. In the 1946 midterm elections, for example, "Republicans 'experimented' with anti-Communism as a political sword wielded against Democratic incumbents and the New Deal," painting the Democrats as "soft on Communism." Richard Nixon and Joseph McCarthy both used fears of communist influence to win elections to the House and Senate. This strategy succeeded, with Republicans gaining twelve seats in the Senate and fifty-five in the House, giving the party control of both houses of Congress. Both parties came away from this election with a sense that red-baiting was good for politics. Historians of McCarthyism, including Stanley Kutler, Schrecker, and Belknap, also stress the importance of domestic political culture. In these works, the Cold War's impact is not a "wartime" impact. Instead, during the early years of the Cold War, international threats informed domestic political cleavages, and national security became a tool of partisan politics.[37]

The possibility that the domestic politics of security had a greater impact on rights than the external threat itself is supported by recent work on public opinion during war.

The political scientist Adam Berinsky argues that wartime public opinion is determined by the same factors as during other times. War and crisis in the abstract are not what affect public opinion, at least in a sustained way over time. Rather, Berinsky argues, the American public's reaction to war is mediated through domestic politics and interest groups, in the same way the public's perceptions of domestic matters are. Although dramatic events like Pearl Harbor can directly affect public opinion, it is "primarily structured by the ebb and flow of partisan and group-based political conflict." This happens during war and peace. "Moreover," Berinsky argues, "we can better understand critical public choices during times of international conflict—notably, support for civil liberties and the election of political leaders—by looking to the same factors that shape opinion on the domestic stage."[38] Berinsky helps us to see that there is a filter between war and the domestic reaction: the construction of narratives of war by political elites, sometimes in partisan ways. In this way, domestic and often partisan political discourse can be more important to public opinion on military conflict than international events themselves.

This insight helps to explain the disconnect, described above, between the period of civil liberties repression and the path of Cold War international relations. The domestic politics of security are not simply generated by the outside— by global tension that travels, unmediated, into the domestic sphere—but by a fusion of domestic and international, as the Cold War became a feature of domestic politics. "National security has been influenced by the same dynamics as all other issues," the historian Julian Zelizer writes. "Partisanship, inter-branch struggles, . . . electoral competition, and more," help to constitute the national security politics that sometimes impact civil liberties. A reason that the impact of the Cold War on civil liberties did not track geopolitical tensions is that geopolitics informed but did not determine the domestic politics of repression.[39]

A further complication is that some rights became stronger, not weaker, during the early Cold War years. Civil rights of African Americans and other racial minorities improved somewhat. Civil rights activists were often red-baited and their activities restricted, but the Supreme Court held that racial segregation in public schools was unconstitutional, and Congress passed landmark civil rights legislation. During these years, global attention was focused on race discrimination in the United States, and American leaders believed that widespread global criticism of segregation harmed U.S. foreign affairs, so that equality rights were directly tied to international relations. A body of scholarship demonstrates that Cold War–era foreign affairs aided domestic civil rights reform through the mid-1960s.[40]

Although scholarship on both civil rights and civil liberties argues that the Cold War affected rights, only the former relies on foreign relations sources. Drawing from such materials, civil rights historians are able to make direct connections between rights and Cold War geopolitics. There is more to it than timing. In spite of these important methodological differences, however, these works are often conflated by scholars seeking to characterize rights generally in the Cold War era, as if they were demonstrating a causal impact from the same source.[41]

The Cold War had an impact on rights not because the era was warlike, with a start, a finish, and repression in the middle. Different rights map onto different time lines, some geopolitical, others domestic. The early Cold War era encompassed two things at the same time: a foreign-relations climate in which the American global image was important, thereby facilitating some civil rights reform; and a domestic climate in which international affairs fueled a red scare that became a powerful feature of domestic politics.

UNLIMITED WAR AND SOCIAL CHANGE

If times of war can drive social change, what do we make of the first "hot war" of the Cold War years? The Korean War, which never formally ended, has been called "the Forgotten War." It has largely eluded the attention of scholars interested in war and civil liberties, and it is most often collapsed into the Cold War period, as compared with Vietnam, which is analyzed on its own. Korea matters not only because it was an important military engagement that had a major impact on both domestic American politics and international affairs. Korea was also the first major military conflict of the Atomic Age, and exemplified the kind of warfare the United States would engage in for the rest of the twentieth century. It was a limited war. Modern limited war, the military historian Adrian Lewis argues, is "an artificial creation caused by the development of nuclear weapons." One of the driving dynamics of the war was what American leaders sought to avoid: all-out war with the Soviet Union.[42]

World War II liberated Korea from Japanese occupation. American and Soviet forces occupied it after the war, with Americans in the south and Soviets in the north, divided by the 38th parallel. This was meant to be a temporary postwar arrangement. However, by 1948, as U.S.-Soviet relations deteriorated, the border became a militarized boundary. In August 1948, the Republic of South Korea was formed, followed a few weeks later by the Democratic People's Republic of Korea in the north. Expecting that the United States would not intervene, North Korean forces invaded the south on June 25, 1950, with the aid of Soviet advisors and equipment. These developments shocked Truman. The newly established United Nations Security Council quickly passed a resolution calling for support to repel the invasion (the Soviet Union was boycotting the Security Council, and therefore wasn't present to veto the measure). Meanwhile, North Korean forces pushed South Korean forces to Pusan, at the southern end of the Korean peninsula. Believing that the stakes in Korea included "the ominous threat of a third world war," Truman committed American ground troops. Three years and millions of civilian and military casualties later, the Americans, Soviets, and North and South Koreans had settled into an ongoing stalemate near the point it had all begun: the 38th parallel.[43]

During the Korean War, the historian Susan A. Brewer writes, "the Truman administration confronted a problem its successors would face in future wars: how to persuade Americans that they were fighting for the highest stakes in a limited war in a small faraway country about which they knew nothing." Public relations had long been an element of U.S. war policy. During World Wars I and II, the government relied on temporary war-related agencies for public relations campaigns. After World War II, "instead of calling

U.S. Marines file past a burning building in Kojo, North Korea, November 2, 1950. Bettman/CORBIS.

upon poets, historians, and artists to serve in a temporary wartime agency," the U.S. government expanded the role of public information departments and officers throughout the executive branch. "As the nation assumed an ongoing state of war," Brewer writes, "government propaganda became permanent and professional." With most of the nation focused on domestic concerns, the Truman administration's efforts sought to reach that part of the American public (according to Brewer, 25%) that followed international affairs. "They courted their support with special briefings and appointments to presidential advisory boards and committees. . . . Officials figured that if these notables endorsed their product the rest of the public would buy it."[44]

The defining U.S. national security objectives in Korea were containing the Soviet Union and avoiding a nuclear apocalypse. Korean territory, like the Pusan peninsula, was important as a site of conflict over communism. By defining Korea as a battle to stop Soviet aggression, Americans could translate this distant war into something that protected their own neighborhoods. This aligned the Korean conflict with domestic Cold War politics, as congressional investigatory committees did not interrogate North Korean sympathizers, after all, but communist fellow travelers.[45]

The Korean War era produced a landmark Supreme Court ruling: *Youngstown Sheet and Tube v. Sawyer* (1952), also called the Steel Seizure Case, which set constitutional limits to presidential war power. But like the anticommunist cases, *Youngstown* ultimately fails to illuminate the relationship between Cold War geopolitics and constitutional power. The case grew out of a labor dispute. Following unsuccessful efforts to negotiate a wage increase, the United Steel Workers Union of America called for a nationwide strike in April 1952. Truman issued an executive order, enabling the federal government to seize the mills and keep them operating. The president was concerned about the effect of a steel strike on the availability of war materiel, yet was also unwilling to use other means to block a strike that might anger labor, a key Truman constituency. The Supreme Court took the *Youngstown* case on an expedited basis and overturned Truman's order.[46]

In accounts of presidential power and wartime, this case stands for the proposition that there are limits to presidential power, even during war. The basis for Truman's exercise of power had parallels in Roosevelt's argument in the years before World War II was declared that he had broad commander-in-chief powers. But there seemed no limit to the Truman administration's argument that the president has inherent power in an emergency. In a 6–3 vote, the Court rejected that position, and Justice Robert Jackson wrote a concurrence that would inform analyses of presidential power in later years, arguing that the scope of presidential power varied depending on whether the president acted in accordance with or against Congressional grants of power. *Youngstown* would be viewed as an important example of the way presidential power could be constrained during wartime, although the legal scholars Louis Fisher and Neal Devins argue that it would not lead the Court to limit presidential initiatives in future cases.[47]

Even as the Steel Seizure Case was unfolding, a more important Cold War–related shift in favor of executive branch power was underway. "America's Cold War changed shape after 1950," the political scientist Campbell Craig and historian Fredrik Logevall explain. "It became a global campaign, much more ideologically charged, far more expensive—the military budget shot up from $14 billion in 1949 to $53 billion in 1953—and a substantially greater factor in the lives of ordinary Americans." An engine of this change was a new and more alarmist conception of national security. In the aftermath of a successful Soviet test of a nuclear weapon and of the "fall" of China in 1949, Truman asked the Departments of State and Defense for an assessment of American national security policy. The result was NSC-68, a report on United States Objectives and Programs for National Security, a document that the international relations scholar Andrew Bacevich notes would be seen "as one of the foundational documents of postwar American statecraft."

In alarmist tones, the report argued that the world was at a crisis point. "The Soviet Union, unlike previous aspirants to hegemony, is animated by a new fanatic faith, antithetical to our own, and seeks to impose its absolute authority over the rest of the world." In a world dominated by two superpowers, the United States needed to respond to this threat by asserting world leadership to combat communism anywhere in the world. This required an ambitious program of building American military capacity. President Truman initially resisted, hoping to keep the federal budget in check, but reversed course with the war in Korea.[48]

This highly ideological cast on the Cold War set the nation on a course of massive military build-up, and what many see as an overreaction to the Soviet threat, committing the nation to worldwide military engagement. These developments resulted in part from the nature of a bipolar world in which the superpowers gained strength not from alliances but from building up their own capacities. But the full extent of American reaction wasn't explained by security needs, Craig and Logevall suggest. Truman went further than he needed to in greatly expanding the military budget, in American actions in Korea, and in political repression at home.[49]

The fuller explanation for the scope of the American overreaction to the Cold War was that "crusading anti-communism became intimately bound up with practical politics. Candidates for office learned quickly that opposing radicals and the Soviet Union was the sine qua non of effective campaigning." In this environment, "the range of acceptable political debate narrowed sharply." Craig's and Logevall's analysis resonates with the work of those historians who see the McCarthy era as a product of complex domestic political dynamics rather than a direct "wartime" impact. The Cold War turn in American politics went far beyond the repression of civil liberties, however. Many interests were served by a more vigorous Cold War strategy. "Just as the New Deal created an array of institutions and interests that saw their prosperity and even their existence tied to the ever-growing expansion of the American state, the Cold War did the same thing after 1950 in the arena of foreign policy, though on a greater scale." Ultimately, "a permanent defense establishment was coming into being."[50]

Legal scholars studying the impact of war and war-making on American domestic institutions tend to focus on how this era compares with other war eras, not on the development of the national security state. They measure the domestic consequences, comparing disputes over rights and presidential power during the Korean War and/or the Cold War with other wartimes.[51] But traditional American wartimes don't offer the right kind of comparison. The Cold War is not an impact on American democracy that began with an opening battle and ended with an armistice. Instead it was a period of state-building akin to the New Deal era. During both periods, the United States embraced a new logic of governance. New institutional structures and economic relationships flowed from these shifts in governance. Once in place, many had an interest in their continuance.

"We have been compelled to create a permanent armaments industry of vast proportions," Eisenhower said in a speech marking his retirement from the presidency. This "military-industrial complex" was needed to respond to security threats, but it was also "new in the American experience."

As Eisenhower put it, "The total influence—economic, political, even spiritual—is felt in every city, every statehouse, every office of the federal government." He warned that the nation "must guard against the acquisition of unwarranted influence, whether sought or unsought, by the military industrial complex. The potential for the disastrous rise of misplaced power exists and will persist." Years later, members of Congress continue to support military spending, in part hoping to bring bases and military contracts to their districts. Military spending has been funded by borrowing, which, Craig and Logevall argue, "subsidiz[ed] military industries to the point that entire regions of the country became economically dependent on them." More important has been the "militarization of American politics" as "each generation of politicians in Washington rediscovered the winning political formula of talking tough on communists."[52]

The nation's global war against communism would mean that military engagements continued, but these battles did not take on the Soviets directly, but were carried out on the periphery. American military intervention in Lebanon in 1958 and 1982–1983, the Dominican Republic in 1965–1966, Grenada in 1983–1985, and elsewhere was limited in scope, so the American people rarely felt that they were at war. The historian Marilyn Young argues that post–World War II administrations "had to create a public tolerance for war as normal rather than aberrational, so normal that after a while only those who were actively engaged in fighting it—and their families—noticed it was being fought at all."[53]

For legal scholars, however, the development of the national security state has either been largely conceded or simply ignored. The *Youngstown* case, nevertheless, remains the focus of histories of the Constitution and the war powers during the Korean War, directing our attention to one arena of conflict over presidential power—the courts—when the real story of the growth of executive power lay elsewhere. Since that time, with some exceptions, legal scholars have largely focused on *Youngstown*-like questions about whether the Court can rein in presidents. In this way, the great constitutional battle over presidential power during the Korean War simply serves as a distraction.

When scholars work to fit the Cold War into the model of traditional wartimes, they obscure the crucial and continuing way a state structure was built. Many persist in calling the structure of American government in the late twentieth and early twenty-first centuries the "New Deal state," reinforcing the idea that the changes in the structure of government that matter most stemmed from the 1930s. But a national security state was built on the New Deal foundation, and as global Cold War commitments drained more and more of the nation's resources, the national security state would be the most important threat to the survival of what remained of the New Deal in the twenty-first century. [55]

Meanwhile the Korean War's impact is often lost, folded into a longer, colder conflict. In national security politics, Korea was the moment when the question of whether the nation was on a permanent war footing was answered in the affirmative. And Korea's importance for examining war and social change is that it helps us to focus on the dynamic that would drive domestic reaction to war through the rest of the century. Alongside a permanent arms industry was now an ongoing effort to manage public opinion. And as political figures took up war and security in domestic political battles, they helped to produce the understanding of war that most Americans experienced.

As we will see in the next chapter, this would prove to be important in the early years of the twenty-first century, when buildings fell in Manhattan, and an American president declared war on terrorism.

4

What Is a War on Terror?

ON SEPTEMBER 11, 2001, COUNTLESS people in the United States and around the world were thrown together in time as they watched the effects of the terrorist attacks unfold on television. The shocking sight of an airplane exploding into the World Trade Center in New York City was, for many, a replay of news footage. But images of the WTC towers collapsing were seen in "real time" by millions who, upon hearing news of the terrorist attacks, turned on their TVs.

The television was on that day in a waiting room at the Veterans Administration hospital in Indianapolis, Indiana; a hotel lobby in Eugene, Oregon; the Coast Guard operations center in Chesapeake, Virginia; at the offices of the Army Reserve in Oklahoma City, Oklahoma; the Southern Ohio Area Social Security Administration; and the North Carolina Division of Emergency Management in Raleigh; at fire departments in Austin, Texas, and Waukegan, Illinois; and at the Utah State Prison. People watched TV alone or together in homes, schools, and workplaces around the country and around the world: at Walgreens; on a large auditorium screen at a conference in Maryland; in a college Common Room at Oxford University in England; in the airport waiting lounge in Shannon, Ireland. Derrick C. Blohm in Chicago called his mother-in-law in Las Vegas and told her to turn on the television. Jodi Fayard was on her way home from the Home Depot in Daphne, Alabama, when her husband reached her and "almost hollered" over her cell phone for her "to get home and turn the TV on." Deb Young switched on the television while housecleaning at a client's home. A company president not far from the Pentagon in Arlington, Virginia, told employees to turn off the television after the second plane hit the World Trade Center "because people would find it distracting and keep them from their work."[1]

At the Academy of the Sacred Heart, in Omaha, Nebraska, the British Literature teacher burst into Kiley Clemens's French class while she was taking a test, and turned on the television. Bethany, a high school student elsewhere, was at the bottom of the pool in her scuba diving class. "When I came back up, pretty much all of the kids were out of the pool and in my teacher's office watching his TV." The principal at Colin Riebel's high school ordered that the televisions be turned off at midday, but "we, the students, revolted. We argued this was a huge part of our history and we had a right to know what was happening to our country. The school complied and let us watch the news again." A Girl Scout Troop in Wichita, Kansas, spent their meeting that night sitting around a kitchen table, watching the news on TV.[2]

The footage was broadcast "live," meaning at the same time, so what was perceived as the genuine character of the experience came from temporality, not from proximity. Even so, live coverage was interspersed with footage of the second plane smashing into WTC Tower 2, shown over and over. John L. Clark watched with his coworkers as the towers fell, "knowing that there were still hundreds of people in the towers either unaware of the happenings or unable to leave." For those who first heard on the radio, the news was confusing. Some wondered if it was real, or another *War of the Worlds*, the Orson Welles radio play (adapted from H. G. Wells's novel) about an invasion from outer space that terrified listeners in 1938. For Ted L. Glines, who watched as he worked at the front desk of his hotel, the TV coverage initially looked "like something out of a video game. At first, there was no sense of reality to it." But then "those little bitty people (the ones who jumped from the top floors) were shown falling outside the Towers. Such tiny dots; were they really people? That is when the horror of it finally set in. I watched and watched for hours as the scenes were replayed and replayed, and replayed again and again."[3]

Those watching on television sometimes felt that the crowds fleeing from the WTC were somehow less conscious of what was happening, lacking access to immediate TV news coverage. "I often (still after all this time), wonder if they knew," Deb Young, who watched while housecleaning, said of those in the WTC buildings. As Kenneth Summers escaped on a ferry, "I did not look back towards the city and was unaware that WTC 2 had collapsed." Hospitalized with burns, "it would be two more weeks before my wife and daughter would inform me of what really happened that day." Sometimes immediate experience was mixed with television coverage. Debra Baron was in the cafeteria at World Trade Center 7 when "all of a sudden, this woman I knew ran and hid by her cash register hysterically crying, pointing to the window." Baron looked and saw "a plane wing falling from the sky, debris hitting the ground, pieces of the building falling from the sky. . . . Then the TVs in the cafeteria went on, we saw a picture of the one tower on fire." Herbert Ouida escaped from the 77th floor of WTC Tower 1, but his son Todd, on the 105th floor, did not. On his long walk to safety, Ouida heard that

People flee the World Trade Center site after the collapse of the towers, September 11, 2001. Associated Press; Photograph by Gulnara Samoilova.

the towers had fallen, but "did not believe it until I got to 75th Street at my daughter's apartment and saw what happened on TV."[4]

Far from the danger, those watching it on television experienced horror nonetheless as the unthinkable unfolded and thousands died, while the distance of the camera and the cloud of debris obscured the details. There was no distance, of course, in lower Manhattan that morning. Felice Chaifetz emerged from the subway to see "an airplane engine right in front of the entrance to 100 Church Street" where she worked. "Eyeglasses, briefcases, shoes, bloody injured people," were all around her. "And then I looked up to see my fiancé's building in flames." When the first tower fell, "we heard this tremendous roaring sound and a cloud of smoke with a feeling of an earthquake shaking the building."[5]

In World Trade Center 7, Debra Baron remembers, "there was a HUGE explosion, the whole building shook, glass started to partially shatter. The screaming went right through you, the lights were flickering and no one knew what the fuck was going on." As she escaped with a friend, "we had to duck from the falling debris." Time jumbled up into a mix of incredible speed and stasis. For Baron, "at that moment life was at a stand still, no one could move fast enough. . . . My feet were like concrete blocks, I could not move."[6]

Many felt at the time that the moment was historic. "This is the Pearl Harbor of my generation," said Diane Fairben, a school teacher in Queens, New York, whose son, a paramedic, was killed at Ground Zero. Tim McClelland of Winchester, Virginia, who heard the news by instant message, felt the same way. "It has ushered in a new era in American history," said Michael Burke of Bronx, New York, whose brother Billy Burke was a firefighter killed at Ground Zero. Patricia Latessa, a Cincinnati high school teacher, reflected as she watched television about how these scenes would impact her students. "The world they knew was bifurcated, cut in half, a time before and a time after."[7]

The survivors were, like soldiers in battle, caught in an extended present. For television viewers, the day was still unfolding when some began to think about the future. "What are we going to do now, Sir?" a company clerk at Camp Lejeune, North Carolina, asked his Commanding Officer, Major Brian E. Gard. "I knew everyone in the office wanted an answer," Gard later recalled. Upset by the news, he "curtly responded 'what do you mean, we are going to go about our duties, we are going to continue to train. Let's get back to work.'"[8]

A NEW WARTIME?

Amid the terror and confusion that day was a discomforting narrative ambiguity: What was this? Before September 11, 2001, the words "terrorism" and "war" had not been conflated. They were two categories, two problems that called for different responses. The most similar recent occurrence had been the April 1995 Oklahoma City bombing by Timothy McVeigh, which brought down large sections of the Alfred P. Murrah Federal Building, killing 168 people and injuring hundreds more. A less devastating attack was the 1993 bombing of the North Tower of the World Trade Center in New York. Neither episode initiated a war on terrorists. Both times the perpetrators were arrested, tried, sentenced and punished, with McVeigh's death sentence carried out June 11, 2001.[9]

It was not immediately clear whether events would unfold in a similar way after the September 11 attacks. To observers at home and abroad, however, America itself had been wounded, even though citizens of many nations were killed that day. In an extraordinary moment of global solidarity, peoples of other nations brought flowers and candles to U.S. embassies. At the same time, a fierce debate erupted about how to define what had happened to America, and how the country should respond.[10]

New York Mayor Rudolph Giuliani spoke to the collective grief when he told a reporter that the number of casualties "will be more than any of us can bear." But it was President George W. Bush who ultimately brought narrative closure to this ambiguous moment. On September 11 he spoke of evil acts and of national resolve, but on September 12 he was clearer: "The deliberate and deadly attacks which were carried out yesterday against our country were more than acts of terror," he announced. "They were acts of war." This was "a new kind of war," he added the next day. The perpetrators were not horrific criminals. They were not even terrorists, as that word had been understood before. They were, in essence, a new kind of terrorist, able to make war on the most powerful nation on earth. Placing them in the category of warrior might have ennobled them, but this "new kind of war" was against an enemy that would not warrant the honor or protection that historically a warring nation accorded its foe.[11]

Having framed this era as a wartime, Bush faced the important tasks confronted by other presidents at war. Besides crafting a military response, he needed to rally the country behind him to ensure support for the nation's war aims. Roosevelt did this when he focused the nation's attention on the Japanese attack on Pearl Harbor, when Japan had attacked numerous other sites in the Pacific the same day. Like Roosevelt, Bush used a major address to a joint session of Congress to communicate his vision to the American people. As had American leaders during the Cold War, he imposed traditional categories on an unruly present. Central to government efforts to rally the nation behind this war effort was the need to cast it as a good war worth fighting.[12]

"Tonight, we are a country awakened to danger and called to defend freedom," Bush told Congress and the nation on September 20. "Enemies of freedom committed an act of war against our country." These enemies were a global network of Islamic extremists headed by Osama bin Laden. The goal of this network was nothing less than "remaking the world—and imposing its radical beliefs on people everywhere." Just as NSC-68 had cast the Cold War as a battle against a hostile regime seeking world domination, what President Ronald Reagan called "the evil empire," Bush argued that al Qaeda was a global force opposed to American democratic values.[13]

September 11 initially generated introspection. "One of the most widely asked questions in the weeks and months following the Sept. 11 terrorist attacks," according to Riad Z. Abdelkarim, a communications director for the Council on American-Islamic Relations, was "'Why do they hate us?'—the 'they' in this question ostensibly referring to the world's Arabs and Muslims." For Bush, however, there was no need for self-reflection, for what made the United States an anathema to this enemy was the core of America itself: democracy and freedom of expression. It was not the United States, but these new terrorists, he argued, who had imperial designs. "They want to overthrow existing governments in many Muslim countries, such as Egypt, Saudi Arabia, and Jordan. They want to drive Israel out of the Middle East. They want to drive Christians and Jews out of vast regions of Asia and Africa."[14]

The United States had not retreated in the face of such threats before, and would not now, he insisted. "We have seen their kind before. They are the heirs of all the murderous ideologies of the 20th century. By sacrificing human life to serve their radical visions—by abandoning every value except the will to power—they follow in the path of fascism, and Nazism, and totalitarianism. And they will follow that path all the way, to where it ends: in history's unmarked grave of discarded lies." The United States was defending a war that terrorists waged against the civilized world, and in this struggle, "God is not neutral." Having placed this new threat in the context of past totalitarian efforts that led to global warfare, the president laid the basis for invoking his war powers. How would the nation confront this threat? With "every necessary weapon of war."[15]

Calling the attacks of September 11 an act of war, and characterizing the U.S. response as a war, was a narrative move of great significance. If war had commenced, the nation had entered an exceptional state, a new time-zone when the usual rules would not apply. The American people would surely have accorded the president some form of extraordinary deference and authority in the immediate aftermath of 9/11 in any case. By signaling that a war had begun, the president signaled the beginning of wartime, an era of enhanced presidential power, which would only come to a close when the war came to an end.[16]

If the president seemed to do this to rally public support for the administration's response to the attacks, he was not alone. A war narrative would be reinforced in American popular culture. Although legal scholars would debate whether the era was wartime, they coalesced around a conventional understanding: that there was an ideal of normal time that was periodically ruptured and restored. Whatever title might be ascribed to this new era, it was not normal time.

Plans for a war strategy unfolded quickly behind the scenes in the Bush administration. In the Presidential Emergency Operations Center on the evening of September 11, the president met with his top staff. "We are at war," he told them, "and we will stay at war until this is done." As Richard Clark, chief counterterrorism advisor on the National Security Council, remembers it, Bush insisted that "nothing else matters." As the journalist Jane Mayer and others have documented, the Bush administration consciously operated on what Vice President Richard Cheney called "the dark side." They worked at the "edges of the law," the former head of the Office of Legal Counsel Jack Goldsmith has written. They saw a strategy of stretching legal restrictions as part of a war strategy.[17]

If 9/11 was a break in the historical time line, a day that "changed everything," as media headlines declared, it called for a new politics. In the supercharged post-9/11 environment, Congress responded quickly. Lawmakers did not pass a formal declaration of war, but instead enacted an "Authorization for Use of Military Force" (AUMF), which was treated as an equivalent. The joint resolution authorized the use of force against "nations, organizations, or persons" behind the attacks, and those who had harbored them. The objective of the AUMF was "to prevent any future acts of international terrorism against the United States by such nations, organizations or persons." "War" does not appear in the resolution except through references to the War Powers Act (1973), which governs the executive branch's use of military force.[18]

Invoking the idea of a war on terror, shortly after September 11 Congress also passed the PATRIOT Act, authorizing broad government surveillance of American citizens and others. President Bush also authorized secret warrantless surveillance of Americans' telephone and e-mail communications by the National Security Agency (NSA), without following the already broad authority granted the president under existing statutes. In by-passing existing authority, the president believed that even broader surveillance was needed as part of the war on terror. The Justice Department argued that the authority granted the president under the AUMF gave him power to do this.

"We cannot fight a war blind," William E. Moschella, assistant attorney general, Office of Legislative Affairs, wrote to members of the Senate Select Committee on Intelligence. "Because communications intelligence activities constitute . . . a fundamental incident of waging war," he argued, the president was authorized to monitor enemy communications, even if that meant warrantless wiretapping of American telephones.[19]

In these and other efforts, the concept of "wartime" became an argument supporting actions that many thought went over the line. Pushing the boundaries during military conflict is of course not new in the American experience. In the post-9/11 era, we can see how the idea of wartime worked as a justification in the debate about a particularly contentious issue: the treatment of detainees in the war on terror.

After September 11, the Bush administration needed intelligence to track down those who played a role in the attacks. The United States constructed a prison camp at Guantánamo Naval Base in Cuba, where the U.S. military could detain and question individuals captured in Afghanistan and Iraq and thought to have ties with al Qaeda. Guantánamo is isolated, which would help keep its operations secret and secure. The Bush administration also hoped that by keeping detainees outside of United States boundaries they would also keep them out of American courts, which would lack jurisdiction over them.

But what sort of legal restrictions applied to interrogations of detainees? Torture was prohibited under domestic and international law. But just what constituted torture, and what rules might limit interrogation techniques? The Office of Legal Counsel (OLC), which serves as legal adviser to the White House, addressed these issues in a series of memos. A 2002 memo defined torture itself extremely narrowly. The now-infamous 2003 memo by John C. Yoo, deputy assistant attorney general in the Office of Legal Counsel, took up the question of legal limits on the executive branch. As the legal scholar Marty Lederman put it, the memo "effectively gave the Pentagon the green light to disregard statutory limits on torture, cruelty and maltreatment in the treatment of detainees." Justice Department documents later revealed that CIA operatives had exceeded even the guidelines in the torture memos, using waterboarding 183 times in one month against the September 11 planner Khalid Sheik Mohammed.[20] The justification for these actions was that it was wartime.

In elaborating his reasoning for finding expansive power to engage in extreme interrogations, Yoo repeatedly invoked the idea of wartime. "In wartime," he wrote, "it is for the President alone to decide what methods to use to best prevail against the enemy." The commander-in-chief power included all necessary ancillary powers. And he interpreted prior case-law as according the president "complete discretion." While Yoo insisted that "our analysis here should not be confused with a theory that the Constitution somehow does not 'apply' during wartime," nevertheless, Fifth Amendment due process restrictions "simply do not address actions the Executive takes in conducting a military campaign against the Nation's enemies," and hence did not apply to the detainees. The Eighth Amendment's prohibition on cruel and unusual punishment also did not apply. "Indeed, it has long been established that '[c]aptivity [in wartime] is neither a punishment nor an act of vengeance,' but 'merely a temporary detention which is devoid of all penal character.'"[21]

Invoking wartime as an argument in this way helps us to see that wartime works as a shorthand, invoking the traditional notion that the times are both exceptional and temporary. In this memo it is shorthand applied to legal arguments. For example, the Eighth Amendment protects against excessive punishment, but wartime detention, Yoo argues, is not a punishment because its purpose is not corrective and its duration is determined by the state of war, not the need for retribution or rehabilitation. In this way, Yoo's invocation of wartime brings with it the notion of temporariness. The imprisonment may look and feel the same, but wartime's inherent temporal limit helps place the Guantánamo detainees outside the realm of Eighth Amendment protection. This particular argument focuses on law, not policy or morality, but as Goldsmith has described it, legal arguments became the standard within the Bush administration, essentially supplanting policy arguments and normative arguments.[22] Meanwhile, for those who wished to take up deeper justifications for harsh interrogation, the concept of wartime also worked as a shorthand normative argument. Extreme techniques were justified for two reasons: the circumstances were extraordinary and they were temporary, so any breach of human rights would necessarily be for a limited duration, making it more tolerable.

But the idea of wartime did something more. Bush administration lawyers and policymakers looked to the past for examples, setting their own time within the context of past wartimes. In so doing they could see themselves as part of an inevitable pattern. They were bound by their times to go to the edges of propriety. Wartime was more than a justification; it was an explanation of what fate demanded of them.

From the beginning, September 11 was widely seen as a day that "changed everything." The conflict had broken time, severed historical continuity, and ushered in a new era. Anyone who questioned the need for a broad new government war strategy was engaged in "September 10 thinking." As a war, 9/11 might have been tidier had its scope been restricted to Afghanistan, the nation that harbored al Qaeda and where for years Osama bin Laden was thought to reside. It was the desire to broaden the war to Iraq that made the story harder to follow. In 2002, Congress passed a second and more lengthy joint resolution authorizing military force against Iraq. This resolution explicitly placed the use of force against Iraq in the context of the war on terror. It noted that "Iraq's ongoing support for international terrorist groups combined with its development of weapons of mass destruction" violated U.N. Security Council resolutions. War was traditionally thought to be bounded in space and time. Extending military action to Iraq showed that the war on terror was conceptualized along the lines of the Cold War era: it was a battle against an ideology that could be found anywhere on the globe. Like communism, the new kind of terrorism could pop up anywhere. Once the enemy was not a nation-state or even an identifiable social group, but an ideology, war seemed to have no boundaries in space or time, but seeped into the global spaces where those evil ideas reside.[23]

The most consistent characteristic among the terrorists was their religion. While the Bush administration emphasized that not all Muslims were terrorists, it did seem that all the terrorists were Muslims. But there were good Muslims and bad Muslims. President Bush tried to distinguish the two in a speech at the National Endowment for Democracy in October 2006: "while the killers choose their victims indiscriminately, their attacks serve a clear and focused ideology, a set of beliefs and goals that are evil, but not insane. Some call this evil Islamic radicalism; others, militant Jihadism; still others, Islamo-fascism." It was different from Islam as a religion, Bush argued, and instead exploited the faith "to serve a violent, political vision," and to establish "a totalitarian empire that denies all political and religious freedom."[24]

If Muslims were to be divided into good and bad categories, Saddam Hussein of Iraq was clearly a bad Muslim, and so somehow the dots were connected between Iraq and the "war on terror." Senator Robert Byrd put it this way: "The face of Osama bin Laden morphed into that of Saddam Hussein." He argued that the president "carefully blurred these images in his State of the Union Address." There was never any evidence to tie the al Qaeda attacks with Iraq, but Bob Woodward and others have argued that the president and his advisors had Iraq in their sights from the beginning. British Prime Minister Tony Blair, addressing the British people, and Colin Powell, secretary of state, testifying before the United Nations about a nuclear weapons threat, both added credibility to the idea that Iraq possessed weapons of mass destruction. These weapons would surely be passed from one bad Muslim to another. Faced with the prospect that Saddam Hussein might be stockpiling nuclear weapons materials, and that nuclear material could end up in al Qaeda's hands, Congress lined up behind war with Iraq. It later became clear, however, that no credible evidence supported either of these assumptions.[25]

Although initiated by the United States, the invasion of Iraq was now framed as a "preemptive" war. The idea of preemption enabled American leaders to cast the initiation of war as defensive rather than offensive, to suggest that they were simply disarming a nation with aggressive and destructive intent. If the idea of invasion-as-defense seemed a form of double-speak worthy of Orwell's Big Brother, once troops were on the ground the irony faded from view. By the spring of 2004, most Americans supported the invasion of Iraq, and a poll found that 49 percent believed that "clear evidence that Iraq was supporting al Qaeda has been found." Vice President Cheney continued to insist that evidence of a link between Hussein and Osama bin Laden was "overwhelming," but the report of the National Commission on Terrorist Attacks upon the United States, an official government investigatory panel, found no evidence of collaboration.[26]

The conflation of Iraq and Afghanistan came not only from the Bush administration. It was enabled by the portrayal of September 11 in American popular culture, as the conflict largely devolved into a battle between the United States and militant Islam. Cultural life took on a mournful tone in the immediate aftermath of September 11. Broadway went dark, and professional baseball, the quintessential American pastime, came to a stop. The nation rallied behind the American flag as an icon for memorializing 9/11. Americans could simultaneously move forward, but also "never forget" by sometimes literally wrapping themselves in the flag. For baseball players, the games could open again six days later with the pledge of allegiance and the song "God Bless America," and with American flags on the players' uniforms.[27]

The threat the nation faced seemed amorphous, but it was soon literally given voice. The first feature film treatment was released in April 2006, and concerned the story of the hijacked United Airlines flight that crashed near Shanksville, Pennsylvania, after passengers fought back. Audiences viewing *United 93* knew how the story would turn out before they stepped into the theater. The filmmakers nevertheless created narrative tension before the first image appeared on the screen.[28]

The film opens with an unfamiliar sound. The words are hard to make out but it soon becomes clear that the quiet sound is an Islamic prayer. The first images in the film are also of praying, as the opening scenes cut back and forth between the lives soon to become entwined: the passengers and the flight crew, and five Muslim men, praying. The sound of prayer takes the place usually occupied by a musical score, bringing dramatic tension to otherwise ordinary scenes. A narrative line has already been drawn from the opening prayer to the inevitable ending, with the plane crashing into a field in Pennsylvania, killing everyone on board. In this storyline, invoking Allah leads to terror. The full implications were emphasized in the closing credits to the original version: "America's war on terror had begun."[29]

United 93 is a war story of great ambiguity, and so its importance may be more in the way it memorialized an understanding of a set of historic events rather than in the film's own narrative. In need of heroes, many latched onto the passengers of United flight 93. What happened on that flight can never fully be known. As the film critic Dennis Lim has written, "this unseen event exerted an immediate stranglehold on the national imagination. As was quickly apparent, not least to the president's speech writers, Flight 93 was an eminently marketable legend." "Let's roll," among the final words thought to have been overheard from one of the passengers, became a call for action in the broader war on terror, invoked by the president himself. This message occluded the film's narrative of an unprepared and chaotic government and military that ultimately left individuals to fend for themselves in the first skirmish in a new battle zone. Individual heroism triumphs in spite of, not because of, the nation. And the only victory was death for all, while protecting an iconic building (the U.S. Capitol was thought to be the intended target). The credit line in the final version of the film is stripped of nationalism, and states only that it was "Dedicated to the memory of all those who lost their lives on September 11, 2001." Yet *United 93* is taken as a symbol of America overcoming terrorism.[30]

United 93 was generally lauded for offering an apolitical take on September 11, but the story's frame is consistent with the most important characteristic in the official September 11 war narrative: whatever else it was about, the "war on terror" involved America and Islam. And, as national identity is often framed in response to an enemy, the threat of radical Islam gave Americans a way to see themselves. It is in war that citizens see the state, Randolph Bourne wrote nearly a century ago. The state can consolidate itself, unite its people, understand its own nature, know its own power, in relation to an "other" against whom it is in conflict.[31] A terrifying vision of Islam became a mirror in which we find America.

LAW DURING WAR WITHOUT END

But was the post-9/11 era really a "wartime"? Legal scholars remain divided in their assessments, debating whether "war" or "state of emergency" is the better way to frame the security environment Americans found themselves in. Many adopted a traditional wartime frame and supported an expansion of executive power, emphasizing the need for government action to address the danger. Others countered that the war on terror did not fit the definition of war under international law. This mattered a great deal, since the switch from peace to war triggers the application of the law of war and international human rights protections, including the Geneva Conventions. The constitutional scholar Bruce Ackerman argued that this was not a war, but an "emergency." Before long, "emergency" or "crisis" became dominant ways of describing the post-9/11 era. Looking for historical analogies, some scholars have recharacterized wartimes in American history as "emergency times," and at least one important scholarly paper about the impact of war on American courts was renamed, substituting "crisis" for "war."[32]

Underlying the disagreement about how to characterize the post-9/11 era was the concern that "wartime" called for the suspension of normal restrictions on executive power. But if the new era was a wartime, it seemed to have no temporal limits. Ultimately, the constitutional scholar Mark Tushnet argued that the length of the "war on terrorism" means that it is not a war like World War II, but instead is "more like a condition, . . . more like the war on cancer, the war on poverty, or, most pertinently, the war on crime." It is one thing to suspend the rule of law during a time-limited war. "Suspending it during a more or less permanent condition is quite another."[33]

The search for a definition reveals a broader issue. As during the Cold War era, there was a lack of fit between the conceptual categories of wartime and peacetime, and the geopolitical realities scholars confronted post-9/11. In the past, war was most commonly defined as a conflict between nations, not between a nation and an ideology or what has become known as "non-state actors." By the end of the twentieth century, the state had dropped out of many definitions of war. A war on terror was more expansive still: it was a war against a tactic or an ideology, not a single, easily identifiable entity. And as the boundaries of territory and identity expanded, this conflict also seemed to defy the idea that war was limited in time.

Most legal scholars responded not by jettisoning the old categories, but by renaming and repurposing them. For example, in a 2005 essay, the legal scholars Samuel Issacharoff and Richard H. Pildes described the dividing line not as between wartime and peacetime, but between "normal times" and "times of heightened risk to the physical safety" of citizens.[34] Post-9/11 scholarship has persisted in the assumption that normality is a state of existence outside times of danger. "Wartime" and "peacetime" broke down, but the basic temporal structure (normal times, ruptured by non-normal times) largely remained in place in legal thought, even if it seemed uncertain whether normal times would ever return.

While many drew comparisons between the post-9/11 era and other wartimes, for the legal writer Benjamin Wittes the era had a different character, for the war on terror was "a conflict unlike any that this country has ever faced." For Wittes, it was reasonable for the Bush administration to adopt a war model immediately after 9/11, but later in the decade the war on terror "entered a different phase" in which "traditional warfare ha[s] given way to something more elastic."[35] As September 11 recedes, the nation seems to have entered an ambiguous era, one that is neither wartime nor peacetime. For the most part, however, scholars, courts, and lawmakers continue to employ the old categories, although wartime has been renamed as crisis or emergency time.

One of the more curious turns in post-9/11 scholarship is the embrace of the work of Carl Schmitt, a leading German political theorist who became a member of the Nazi Party in the 1930s. There was a revival of interest in Schmitt before 9/11, but references to his work proliferated in legal scholarship in the aftermath, reinforcing a discourse of exceptionality. Schmitt's most widely invoked quote is that the "Sovereign is he who decides on the exception." This seemed to fit the post-9/11 context perfectly, since President Bush had declared that an exceptional moment—a wartime—had commenced with the September 11 attacks. The work of the Italian philosopher Georgio Agamben, who draws from Schmitt's theory of sovereignty to develop a radical critique of the modern state, has also drawn attention, particularly the idea that states of exception tend to become normalized.[36]

Schmitt's work draws from the experience of Weimar Germany—the post–World War I parliamentary republic that disintegrated with the rise of fascism. For American scholars concerned about unbridled executive power, it serves as an important warning of what can happen when security concerns stemming from war or crisis seep into domestic politics. But the focus on Schmitt reinforces the idea that the post-9/11 years are an exceptional moment. Consistent across this literature is the idea that time changed on September 11, that it has ushered in a new era, requiring different analytical tools to understand it.

Citations to Schmitt in legal scholarship steadily increased. A search of the Westlaw legal periodicals database shows twenty-four citations to Schmitt in 2001, twenty-nine in 2002, fifty-one 2003, and eighty-six in 2009. Although some scholarship engaged Schmitt's political theory more broadly, an increasing number more narrowly invoke the idea that the sovereign is he who declares the exception for the purpose of discussing emergency powers. In 2001, two articles citing Schmitt focused only on the idea of sovereign power, and twenty-two discussed broader aspects of his work. In 2008, nearly half of seventy-five articles focused narrowly on this idea.[37]

Some scholars have objected to the turn to Schmitt. Bruce Ackerman argues that reliance on his work has made discussions of emergency power melodramatic when they need to be taken seriously. For the legal scholar Kim Lane Scheppele, "the institutional elaboration of a new international system that has occurred since Schmitt's time make his ideas seem all the more dangerous, and yet all the more dated." The legal scholars Eric Posner and Adrian Vermeule

Citations to Carl Schmitt in American Legal Scholarship

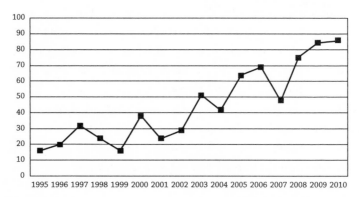

see the embrace of Schmitt as tied to a broader phenomenon—the tendency of scholars to view emergency powers
through "the lens of Weimar." "The specter of Weimar's collapse, in which repeated invocations of emergency powers
were followed by an authoritarian takeover, looms omi-
nously in the civil libertarian imagination." But this has
received too much attention, they argue. "Weimar was an
unconsolidated and institutionally shaky transitional democracy." Its relevance for contemporary democracies,
which tend to be more stable, is limited. Still, Posner and
Vermeule draw from what they consider to be the "marrow"
of Schmitt's ideas, and incorporate them into their analysis
of executive power. Their simultaneous rejection and
embrace of Schmitt illustrates the way references to him
became a language for discussing executive power, even for
those who decried his influence. The turn to Schmitt thus
solidified the idea that the crisis of 9/11 generated a state
of exception, an era when the normal rules of law might
give way to governance through emergency powers.[38]

Taken out of context, as it often is, Schmitt's iconic sentence "can mean almost anything," the Schmitt scholar Ellen
Kennedy argues. His dichotomies, including norm/excep-
tion, "operate now as tropes." While Kennedy's work contex-
tualizes and complicates Schmitt's conception of sovereignty,
the political philosopher John Brenkman argues that even
within the terms of recent scholarship, the idea that sovereign power unravels a rule of law in times of crisis oversim-
plifies. The problem posed by Schmitt's theorem, he argues,
is that it is self-justifying: "since the rule of law rests on the
capacity to suspend the rule of law if necessary, whoever
declares a state of exception will almost inevitably claim that
it is necessary for the preservation of the rule of law and
indeed the body politic itself," even if the claim is specious.[39]

Brenkman argues, however, that claims of emergency do not necessarily lead democracies to unravel. "Political systems can be resiliently self-correcting, especially as the public's sense of emergency wanes or the government's claim of necessity is thrown into doubt." More fundamentally, he argues, Schmitt's formulation of the sovereign as he who declares the exception obscures "the little wedge created by the distinction—and hence the potential gap—between declaration and claim, act and justification, rule and legitimacy." It is here, "along these hairline fractures in the discourse of power" that Brenkman finds "the very possibility of a political realm and of democracy."[40]

Where does this hairline fracture appear in legal thought, and how is it managed? Legal scholars writing about the post-9/11 era, like those who engaged the Cold War and other conflicts, tend to take external events, like wars, as a given. The crisis appears to exist out in the world, outside the realm of law, and it is the legal scholar's task to take up the way those external events affect the law's functioning. The crisis exists, and law reacts until the crisis goes away. This way of thinking is reflected in the current exceptionality discourse, which assumes that we live in a crisis time that differs from normal time. But following from Brenkman, the exception derives not only from something external, but in the wedge between "declaration and claim, act and justification." The need for legitimacy puts the possibility of politics in the middle of the identifying of a state of exception. The crisis isn't external to the world of politics that law occupies. Instead, exceptionality derives from something internal and political: the framing or articulation of crisis, and its justification.

Along that hairline fracture, in that political space, lies the construction of the idea of wartime. It is there that the narrative work is done, framing an episode as a war, and placing it within the legacy of great American conflicts. For all the challenges of George W. Bush's presidency, he succeeded completely in this most fundamental task: rallying the country behind the idea that the nation is at war.

The greatest challenge to the exceptionality thesis was simply the facts on the ground. If the war on terror was a rupture of normal time, it was inherently temporary, and therefore would last only until normal time resumed. As the era pressed on, Americans turned their focus to their daily lives, even as American troops continued to patrol dangerous territory in Afghanistan and Iraq, and as American unmanned war planes bombed targets in Pakistan. For a moment in spring 2011, Americans were jolted to attention with the news that Osama bin Laden, mastermind behind the 9/11 attacks, was killed by Navy Seals in a compound in Pakistan. "Justice has been done," President Barack Obama announced in a late-night televised speech. Crowds poured into the streets, celebrating at the White House in Washington, Ground Zero in New York City, and around the country. Bin Laden's death might have been a bookend to a decade of war, but the United States had already joined NATO efforts to remove the Libyan leader Colonel Muammar el-Qaddafi, while the Pentagon contemplated treating cyberattacks as acts of war warranting the use of military force. Some members of Congress demanded that Obama seek their approval for continued military action in Libya, but did not have enough votes for a resolution. Then, a few weeks after bin Laden's killing, the public's focus was back on domestic matters like the struggling economy.[41]

The experience of the war on terror was confined to its more direct participants. On Guantánamo itself, the absence of clocks to mark time was intended to provoke anxiety, part of a strategy to disorient the prisoners and make them more likely to be responsive to interrogation. "We didn't know the time," said Shafiq Rasul, a British citizen whose detention would be challenged in the Supreme Court. The prisoners knew when to pray by the position of the sun, and they knew the date "because we counted for ourselves and some soldiers would tell us enough to let us slightly keep track, otherwise there was never meant to be any way." At least in some circumstances, prayer time was marked for the prisoners. Katharine Q. Seelye, a *New York Times* reporter shown the camps in January 2002, reported that "five times a day, the call for daily prayers goes out across the camp." A Department of Defense website shows a yellow traffic cone placed in the hallway of Camp Delta marked with a "P," for prayer time. Seelye took prayer times to be a sign of compliance with prisoners' rights under international law, but it was also a form of control. According to Rasul, "sometimes the prayer call would be played five times a day, but then it would be stopped again." And the marking of time came not from a Muezzin who calls Muslims to prayer, or from the sun, or from mechanical time pieces. On Guantánamo, the guards controlled everything, even God's time.[42]

THE SUPREME COURT AND CRISIS TIMES

The seeming lack of end to this era troubled the Supreme Court when it took up post-9/11 cases related to Guantánamo detainees. In a series of decisions, the Court initially framed arguments within the traditional paradigm, assuming that wartime was temporary and its impact on law eventually would wane. But the ongoing character of the war on terror challenged this idea, and eventually this affected the Court's willingness to place limits on executive power even during a time conceptualized as a wartime.

One of the first important cases, *Hamdi v. Rumsfeld* (2004), concerned an American citizen who was apprehended in Afghanistan and detained at Guantánamo before being transferred to the United States and held at a Naval brig in South Carolina. Hamdi was classified as an "enemy combatant," and the Bush administration argued that the president had power to detain such persons without trial for the duration of hostilities. Justice Sandra Day O'Connor, writing the principal opinion in the case for a plurality of four, noted that there was "some debate as to the proper scope" of the term "enemy combatant," but that in this case the enemy combatant was a person the government alleged was "'part of or supporting forces hostile to the United States or coalition partners' in Afghanistan and who 'engaged in an armed conflict against the United States' there." She was troubled, however, by the potentially indefinite character of Hamdi's detention. Her concern was not with "the lack of certainty regarding the date on which the conflict will end," but with "the substantial prospect of perpetual detention." O'Connor observed, "If the Government does not consider this unconventional war won for two generations, and if it maintains during that time that Hamdi might, if released, rejoin forces fighting against the United States, then the position it has taken throughout the litigation of this case suggests that Hamdi's detention could last for the rest of his life."[43]

The Court did not have to face the prospect of endless detention, however, at least not yet. O'Connor found that the war on terror, at that moment, fit within conventional understandings of military conflict, with temporal limits, for there were "active combat operations" against the Taliban in Afghanistan. It was therefore appropriate to detain Hamdi "for the duration of these hostilities." The plurality found, however, that due process required that Hamdi have an opportunity to challenge his detention. "We have long since made clear that a state of war is not a blank check for the president when it comes to the rights of the nation's citizens," O'Connor wrote. Justice Antonin Scalia dissented, arguing that it would only be lawful for the government to hold an American citizen within U.S. territory without trial if Congress suspended the right to habeas corpus, which Congress may do only in times of invasion or rebellion. Alternatively, Hamdi must be tried using the usual procedures in criminal cases.[44]

In another case that term, *Rasul v. Bush*, involving foreign nationals captured in Afghanistan and held at Guantánamo, the Court held that it had power to hear their habeas corpus petition. Timing mattered to Justice Anthony Kennedy, who agreed with the outcome, but not with the majority's reasoning. "As the period of detention stretches from months to years," he wrote in a concurring opinion, "the case for continued detention to meet military exigencies becomes weaker." This case differed from *Hamdi* in that the detainees were not U.S. citizens and were being held outside U.S. borders. This mattered to Justice Scalia, who dissented, joined by Chief Justice William Rehnquist and Justice Clarence Thomas, arguing that noncitizens held outside the United States lacked the ability to invoke the Court's habeas jurisdiction.[45]

Four years later, the problem of temporality seemed more pressing. In *Boumediene v. Bush* (2008), the Court found unconstitutional a statute intending to strip federal courts of jurisdiction over habeas corpus challenges brought by Guantánamo detainees. Most important to the detainee cases was geography—whether the right to habeas corpus applied to individuals imprisoned outside the borders of the nation, since Guantánamo is in Cuban territory and the United States has a long-term lease. In *Johnson v. Eisentrager*, the Court had denied habeas relief to German prisoners of war held in U.S. custody in Germany after World War II. Writing for the majority, Justice Kennedy distinguished *Eisentrager* from *Boumediene* in part because of differences in the likely duration the prisoners would be held in U.S. custody. American control over the German prison was "neither absolute nor indefinite." Although it was lawful to detain those who had fought against the United States "for the duration of the conflict," Kennedy wrote, he was troubled by the new war's lack of boundaries. The present conflict "if measured from September 11, 2001, to the present, is already among the longest wars in American history." One of the reasons habeas corpus was needed was that "the consequence of error may be detention of persons for the duration of hostilities that may last a generation or more." The lack of time boundaries made this conflict different than past wars, Kennedy reasoned. There were great dangers, but "the laws and Constitution are designed to survive, and remain in force, in extraordinary times," he wrote, and "liberty and security can be reconciled . . . within the framework of the law." Justice Scalia, in dissent, focused instead on the danger of a "war with radical Islamists." The Court's ruling would have "disastrous consequences," he argued, and would "almost certainly cause more Americans to be killed."[46]

By the end of the decade, however, the war on terror had less of a hold on American political consciousness. Mid-term election debates in 2010 were not about security, but about unemployment and economic malaise. Fear of Muslims continued to be a feature of American culture, but it had largely moved to the margins, periodically breaking to the surface, as with virulent opposition to proposed construction of an Islamic cultural center two blocks from Ground Zero in New York. In this climate, the war on terror was a less ubiquitous cultural frame, even as military actions extended the geographic scope of American warfare to Pakistan, and the securitization of daily life remained in place, as new body scanners and invasive physical pat-downs were adopted at American airports.[47]

In June 2010, the problem of terrorism was framed as a "war" in one courtroom, while in another it was more plainly a problem of national security and international relations, but not war. On June 21, Faisal Shahzad pled guilty to an attempt to bomb New York's Times Square. Explaining his efforts, Shahzad said that he was a soldier and wanted to strike back at U.S. and NATO forces that had attacked Muslim lands. When asked whether he was concerned that he might harm children, he responded that when American drones drop bombs in Afghanistan and Iraq "they don't see children; they don't see anybody. They kill women, children. They kill everybody. It's a war." He decided to strike back not at a military installation or government office but a focal point of American culture: Times Square.[48]

But at the Supreme Court the same week, the idea of wartime had become more complicated. *Holder v. Humanitarian Law Project*, a case concerning a federal statute criminalizing material support for terrorist organizations, had been set in

the context of the war on terror. The statute prohibited providing "material support or resources" to organizations that
had been found to engage in terrorist activity. Secretary of
State Madeleine Albright had designated the Kurdistan
Workers' Party and the Liberation Tigers of Tamil Eelam as
terrorist groups in 1997. The plaintiffs in this case, two
Americans and six domestic organizations, supported legal
and nonviolent objectives of these groups, and they sought to
provide financial support for the groups' humanitarian activities. They argued that prohibiting them to do so violated
their constitutional rights.[49]

When the case was argued in the Supreme Court on
February 22, 2010, Fox News reported, "It's the War on
Terror against the First Amendment." When the Court's
ruling came down in June, upholding the statute, the legal
scholar Steve Vladeck called it "one of the most significant
legal victories that the government has obtained to date in
the war on terrorism." The reporter Michael Doyle con-
curred, calling the ruling "the year's most anticipated war-
on-terrorism decision." This case did not involve al Qaeda,
or groups with ties to Afghanistan or Iraq, but instead Sri
Lanka and Turkey. But President George W. Bush had
framed the "war on terror" in broad terms, finding it a
global threat defined more by ideology than national
identity.[50]

In this context, it might be expected for the Court to
issue an opinion that invoked wartime, reinforcing the idea
that the balance between government power and individual
rights shifts away from rights and toward the government
during war. But the term "war on terror" does not appear in
the opinions. Chief Justice John Roberts's majority opinion
upholding the statute kept the focus on "foreign terrorist

organizations." He invoked national security and foreign relations, but in contrast to the *Boumediene* case, he did not
situate the case in the context of wartime. The closest the
opinion came was when Roberts invoked the Constitution's
Preamble, which proclaims that the Constitution's purpose
was "in part to 'provide for the common defense,'" and noted
James Madison's statement in Federalist 41 that "[s]ecurity
against foreign danger is . . . an avowed and essential object
of the American Union." When the majority discussed war,
it was to suggest that the dissent's arguments extended too
far. "If only good can come from training our adversaries in
international dispute resolution," Roberts wrote, "presum-
ably it would have been unconstitutional to prevent American citizens from training the Japanese Government on
using international organizations and mechanisms to
resolve disputes during World War II." Justice Stephen
Breyer, in dissent, also suggested that "these cases require
us to consider how to apply the First Amendment where national security interests are at stake," rather than invoking
the problem of rights in wartime.[51]

In finding the case to be framed by national security
concerns short of war, the Court paralleled the new Obama
administration's attempt to step back from the capacious
idea of a war on terror, and instead to confine war-talk to
more focused arenas of military engagement. Backing away
from the frame of "wartime" did not solve all the difficulties, however. The civil liberties scholar David Cole, who
represented the plaintiffs before the Supreme Court, suggested that the Court used "the same sort of deferential
approach that the Supreme Court took to anti-Communist
laws in the early days of the McCarthy era."[52] The Court
retreated from the contradictory conception of a boundless

wartime. But as during the Cold War, the Court appeared to accede to a new security crisis with no visible end-point. Law in this rendering was not wartime law or Cicero's temporary absence of law, for it was a newly configured, peaceless era, a new kind of normal.

THE PROBLEM OF ENDINGS

Perhaps weighted by time, the post-9/11 war narrative began to fracture by the end of the decade. An alternative framing came first from President Obama, who described the era as a wartime, but stopped short of the more expansive "war on terror." The president described the nation as at war not with an ideology but with specific groups in two nations: Afghanistan and Iraq. He had opposed military action in Iraq, and he campaigned on the idea that the United States needed to withdraw in order to focus on the real threat in Afghanistan. Once in office, however, it became clear that managing public perceptions of war was as important to him as it had been to other presidents.

On August 18, 2010, the conflict in Iraq ended, live on NBC. "It's gone on longer than the Civil War, longer than World War II," said the NBC news anchor Brian Williams. "And tonight, U.S. combat troops have pulled out of Iraq." The station and its cable affiliate MSNBC broadcast live footage of Chief Foreign Correspondent Richard Engel, embedded with the 4th Stryker Brigade, as soldiers drove across the border from Iraq into Kuwait. "This has been a historical moment that we have just seen," noted Engle, although the history-making quality of this episode required some explaining. Fifty thousand American troops were remaining in Iraq, fully armed, and reports of American casualties in Iraq would continue.[53]

On MSNBC, Rachel Maddow explained in her reporting from the Green Zone: "Wars end like this. . . . They end with a political settlement." NBC and its cable affiliate had been given an exclusive ability to cover these events, yet this moment's ambiguity seemed to necessitate their insistence that this *really was* an ending of a war. The evidence that this day was historic, however, came only from the reporters' insistence that it was. There were no photographs of the signing of an armistice agreement. There were no dramatic images, such as those of the American pullout from Vietnam, with refugees clambering after a departing helicopter on the rooftop of the U.S. embassy in Saigon. Just troops in trucks. Yet Maddow claimed: "The combat mission is over; the war is over."[54]

Then, on August 31, President Obama announced "the end of combat operations in Iraq" in a televised speech to the American people. As mid-term elections neared, the president sought to turn attention to domestic matters, including a struggling economy. He called it a "historic moment," coming after "nearly a decade of war." Obama persisted in a rhetorical effort to downplay the war on terror. Rather than casting the many years of conflict as a wartime in which the nation battled a militant form of Islam, he invoked a more limited set of ideas. In Obama's words, President Bush had simply "announced the beginning of military operations in Iraq." Compared to Bush's fiery rhetoric at the opening of the Iraq campaign, Obama's description seemed technocratic and his delivery dispassionate. He seemed more bureaucrat than war leader. It was as if, rather than

Iraqi and U.S. forces take part in a joint raid outside the city of Kirkuk, Iraq, December 24, 2010, after the "end of combat operations in Iraq" was announced. Marwan Ibrahim/AFP/Getty Images.

declaring an end to violent warfare, he was announcing the close of a bloodless government program.[55]

Although the nation's unity was tested during this era, Obama argued, there was one constant: "At every turn, America's men and women in uniform have served with courage and resolve." American troops had "completed every mission they were given." The nature of that mission seemed obscure, but once deployed, the personalization of American war support by the president and others meant that the nation could rally behind its soldiers without engaging the war's broader purpose. The pullout of the last combat brigade was simply "a convoy of brave Americans, making their way home." About the members of the Fourth Stryker Brigade who had "made the ultimate sacrifice," Obama offered a quote from a staff sergeant who had told him equivocally: to them, "This day would probably mean a lot."[56]

Even as Obama announced that the American combat mission in Iraq had ended, he also said that troops would remain—"with a different mission." Just how different the mission would be was clarified when practical questions surfaced, such as, if combat was over, would American troops no longer be eligible for hostile fire pay, or for combat service medals? The army responded with a message to all troops: The "end to combat operations in Iraq" was effective September 1, 2010. However, the army added, "combat conditions are still prevalent," and so wartime awards would "continue to be issued in theater, until a date to be determined." Other combat-service benefits would also still be available. "It is unusual for the Army to come right out and say the emperor has no clothes," noted the journalist Thomas E. Ricks, "but I think it had to in this case, because soldiers take medals seriously." An internal memo from the Associated Press simply rejected the White House message. "Whatever the subject, we should be correct and consistent in our description of what the situation in Iraq is," read the AP memo. "To begin with, combat in Iraq is not over, and we should not uncritically repeat suggestions that it is, even if they come from senior officials. The situation on the ground in Iraq is no different today than it has been for some months."[57]

Perhaps the paradoxical nature of this ending that was not an ending explains the absence in Obama's speech of the president's usual rhetorical power. Grasping for metaphors, he emphasized that American troops were "the steel in our ship of state. And though our nation may be traveling through rough waters, they give us confidence that our course is true, and that beyond the pre-dawn darkness, better days lie ahead." And so the mission had devolved to supporting the troops, while the troops themselves gave the mission meaning. The circularity befitted what the president called "an age without surrender ceremonies;" an age when conflict could end, even as it remained ongoing.[58]

There was one thing the debate about the war's ending was powerless to do: to bring military conflict to an end. New waves of deployment continued, while at home the culture of war fractured further. The Hurt Locker, a film based on the experience of American soldiers in Iraq, was celebrated and criticized for its portrayal of the narcotic effect of the war experience. The film follows a munitions team through the harrowing task of defusing bombs. The film's politics were implicit and indirect, intensifying the era's tendency to bypass the politics of warfare through the focus on individual soldiers. A leader of a U.S. Army Explosive Ordnance Disposal unit lives life on the edge in the film's high-tension scenes. Viewers can only hope that he survives it, to return to the home front and a more normal life. But the high-voltage life of the bomb squad unfits the film's hero for any other life. A visit home shows him out of place outside the war zone. He is drawn to return.[59]

The final scene of *The Hurt Locker* is a metaphor for the American experience with war. Of his own accord, the soldier is again in Iraq, walking cautiously toward the next IED. Like his country, he no longer knows life outside the war zone. War had become normal life. There is terrible danger that it will all end badly. But neither this metaphoric soldier, nor the nation, turns away.

The homefront, in the film and in twenty-first century American culture, was a different world. Absent was the national unity that might be hoped for in a wartime.

Instead, a newly caustic partisanship took hold, so that routine matters like the federal debt ceiling became an arena for partisan brinkmanship. The focus on domestic politics did not serve to lessen the nation's military reach, however, but enabled its expansion. Military engagement no longer seemed to require the support of the American people, but instead their inattention.

Conclusion

THE FIRST DECADE OF THE twenty-first century came to a close during a strange kind of wartime. Barack Obama, like presidents before him, used the holiday season to reflect on American values. Presidents have often used the annual tree-lighting ceremony as an occasion to place the challenges of their era in the context of American history. In December 2011, Obama recalled an earlier Christmas, just weeks after Pearl Harbor, when Franklin Roosevelt stood beside Winston Churchill and lighted the nation's tree. How could Americans "put the world aside" for a day as they had in peaceful years, Roosevelt asked. The answer was that Americans would engage in a particular kind of readiness: "The preparation of our hearts; the arming of our hearts." Once Americans had readied themselves for what lay ahead— "the labor and the suffering and the ultimate victory"—they would know the true meaning of Christmas.[1] The national Christmas tree would then go dark for four years.

Later presidents have used the same occasion to rally the nation, placing war and peace at the heart of the American mission. In doing so, they crafted their times, often placing their moment in the chronology of wartimes. "We create the temporal modes that we inhabit," Thomas M. Allen writes in *A Republic of Time*.[2] And American leaders have used public occasions to help craft shared national times of wartime and peacetime. This helps us to see that "wartime" is not outside of everyday life, a part of an external world which law and politics must adjust to. It is an idea, or a narrative frame, that we craft to make sense of our experience.

We can see this in public celebrations during Cold War Christmases, when presidents did not rally the nation behind a "good war," but invoked American arms in the cause of peace, so that the Cold War's particular fusion of wartime and peacetime was regularly on display. The tree-lighting ceremony was renamed the Pageant of Peace in 1954. For President Dwight D. Eisenhower, the holidays were "a season of hope," even though "the times are so critical," as the nation faced a Cold War struggle between two different ways of life. President Richard M. Nixon spoke of peace and of power when lighting the tree in 1969, for without a strong American role in the world, other nations "could not have peace, except the kind of peace that suffocates freedom." Peace had become a justification for militarization; it could not exist without war as its constant companion.[3]

President George W. Bush used the tree-lighting ceremony in December 2001 to frame American warfare as a form of peacemaking, as he would in pressing for an invasion of Iraq. "America seeks peace and believes in justice. . . . We fight so that oppression may cease, and even in the midst of war, we pray for peace on Earth and good will to men." Bush also praised Americans for carrying on with their daily lives—"working and shopping and playing, worshiping at churches and synagogues and mosques, going to movies and to baseball games." Rather than sacrificing for the war effort, we were to continue with daily life. This reinforced the sense that war was the government's task, and was not something that citizens must take responsibility for.[4]

Although President Obama invoked wartime in his reference to that solemn tree-lighting in 1941, he characterized our own times as only holiday times, in which "we try our hardest to live with a spirit of charity and goodwill."

And then he kept his focus on American soldiers, rather than on the tasks they were seeking to accomplish. In a televised message, the president lauded "our courageous countrymen serving overseas." Gone was the ideology of the past, but gone also was Roosevelt's sense of national purpose. He said nothing of the reasons America was still at war. The labors of American soldiers were no longer cast as part of a global mission, even as the global reach of the American military expanded. War had become personalized, even as its objectives were harder to see.[5]

In Iraq and Afghanistan, war continued and spread across borders as American drones fired on targets in Pakistan and elsewhere. Death and destruction were the province of soldiers and of peoples in faraway lands. The experience of wartime for most Americans largely devolved to encounters between travelers and airport screeners, as the Transportation Security Administration adopted intrusive new practices. At home, wartime had become a policy, rather than a state of existence.

As war governance took on the character of bureaucratic management, rather than crusade, the passion of the Bush years nearly seemed more satisfying. President Bush had taken a national tragedy, and framed it as a new kind of wartime. As a wartime without boundaries, the war on terror broke the problem of war's temporality into the open, revealing anxiety over the impact of perpetual war on American democracy itself. Americans disagreed deeply about this war, but coalesced around the idea that the times were not normal times. As war goes on, Americans have lapsed into a new kind of peacetime. It is not a time without war, but instead a time in which war does not bother everyday Americans.

Meanwhile, threats of terrorism still serve as a justification for enhanced surveillance at home, and for extending the reach of American military action. Wartime continues to be invoked as an argument for extraordinary governance. Once we understand that political actors help to generate a shared political time, we can better see that we are not driven by our times, but instead shape them. Exceptional moments do not by themselves create or necessitate exceptional policies. Instead, as John Brenkman suggests, "between declaration and claim, act and justification, rule and legitimacy" lies the realm of politics. It is along these "hairline fractures in the discourse of power" that we make choices. Wartime is the claim or justification drawn upon for expanding government power. When we understand that "wartime" is an argument, rather than an inevitable feature of our world, then we can see that it need not cause us to suspend our principles. Our times do not determine our actions, they do not absolve us from judgment.[6]

Keeping the war powers in check requires a politics of war, and that requires a citizenry attentive to the exercise of military power.[7] A cultural framing of wartimes as discrete and temporary occasions, destined to give way to a state of normality, undermines democratic vigilance. Thinking of wartime as determining our actions, rather than as an urgent occasion for politics, impedes public engagement and responsibility. To take seriously war's presence as an ongoing feature of American democracy, a starting point is to cease viewing the nation's history as divided into time zones, and to look instead for war's enduring mark on American politics and American law.

APPENDIX

U.S. Military Campaign Service Medals

This chart lists U.S. Military Campaign Service Medals cataloged in John E. Strandberg and Roger James Bender, *"The Call of Duty": Military Awards and Decorations of the United States of America*, 2nd ed. (San Jose, CA: R. James Bender Publishing, 2004). Campaign service medals are meant to recognize service in American military engagements. The chart on page 29 is limited to medals for military campaigns against armed opposing forces and for military occupation. Some medals on this fuller list are for noncombat service. Campaign service medals were first created by Congress in 1906 and recognize military service from the Civil War on. They illustrate that the United States has been engaged in a greater number of military deployments, covering more of American history, than is often recognized. Medals listed in this appendix are organized by region and by branch of service and appear in the order in which they are listed in Strandberg and Bender.

	Service	Begin Date	End Date	Location	Campaign
Civil War					
	Army	4/15/1861	4/9/1865		Civil War Campaign
	Army	4/15/1861	8/20/1866	Service in Texas	Civil War Campaign
	Navy + Marines	4/15/1861	4/9/1865		Civil War Campaign
Indian Wars					
	Army	1865	1891		Indian Campaign
		1865	1868	Oregon, Idaho, California, Nevada	
		1867	1875	Comanches	
		1872	1873	Modoc War	
		1873		Apaches	
		1876	1877	Cheyennes and Sioux	
		1877		Nez Percee	
		1878		Bannoc War	
		1878	1879	Northern Cheyennes	

Branch				Campaign
	6/1879	10/1879	Sheep Eaters, Piutes, Bannocks	
	1879	1880	Utes	
	1885	1886	Apaches	
	1890	1891	Sioux	
	1865	1891	any hostile action	
Spanish American War				
Navy and Marines	2/15/1898	8/13/1898		West Indies Campaign
Navy and Marines	2/15/1898	8/13/1898		Spanish Campaign
Army	5/11/1898	7/17/1898	Cuba	Spanish Campaign
	7/24/1898	8/13/1898	Puerto Rico	
	6/30/1898	8/16/1898	Philippines	
Army	4/20/1898	4/11/1899		Spanish War Service
Army	7/18/1898	5/20/1902		Army of Cuba Occupation Medal
Army	8/14/1898	12/10/1898		Army of Puerto Rico Occupation

(continued)

	Service	Begin Date	End Date	Location	Campaign
Philippines	Army	2/4/1899	7/4/1902	service ashore	Philippine Campaign
		2/4/1899	12/31/1904	Mindanao	
		7/20/1906	6/30/1907	Leyte	
		8/2/1904	6/30/1907	Samar	
		4/1905	5/1905	Pala	
		10/1905		Mindanao	
		3/1906		Jolo	
		1/1913	7/1913	Jolo	
		1/1910	1/1913	Jolo, Mindanao	
		2/4/1899	12/31/1913	any action	
	Navy and Marines	2/4/1899	3/10/1906		Philippine Campaign
	Army	2/4/1899	7/4/1902		Philippine Congressional Medal
China	Army	6/20/1900	5/27/1901		China Campaign
	Navy and Marines	5/24/1900	5/27/1901		China Relief Exp. Medal

Cuba	Army	10/6/1906	4/1/1909		Army of Cuban Pacification
	Navy and Marines	9/12/1906	4/1/1909		Cuban Pacification Medal
Nicaragua	Navy and Marines	7/29/1912	11/14/1912		Nicaraguan Campaign
Mexican Campaign	Army	4/24/1914	11/26/1914	Vera Cruz	Mexican Service Medal
		11/1/1915	11/5/1915	Nogales, AZ	
		3/14/1916	2/7/1917	Punitive Exp. in Mexico	
		12/1/1917		Buena Vista	
		12/26/1917		San Bernardino Cyn.	
		1/8/1918	1/9/1918	Le Grulla, TX	
		3/28/1918		Pitares	
		8/27/1918		Nogales, AZ	
		6/15/1919	6/16/1919	El Paso, TX; Juarez	

(continued)

Service	Begin Date	End Date	Location	Campaign
	4/12/1911	2/7/1917	any action	
Navy and Marines	4/21/1914	4/23/1914	Vera Cruz	Mexican Service Medal
	4/21/1914	11/26/1914	general	
	3/14/1916	2/7/1917	general	
Army and National Guard	5/9/1916	3/24/1917		Mexican Border Service Medal
Texas Cavalry Brigade	1/1/1916			
	12/8/1917	4/6/1917		TX Cavalry Congressional Medal
Haiti				
Navy and Marines	7/9/1915	12/6/1915		Haitian Campaign 1915
Dominican Republic				
Navy and Marines	5/16/1916	12/4/1916		Dominican Campaign

WWI	All Armed Forces	4/6/1917	11/11/1918		World War I Victory Medal
Germany	Army, Navy and Marines	11/12/1918	7/11/1923	Germany or Austria Hungary	Army of Occupation of Germany
Haiti	Navy and Marines	4/1/1919	6/15/1920		Haitian Campaign Medal 1919-1920
Nicaragua	Navy and Marines	8/27/1926	1/2/1933		Second Nicaraguan Campaign
China	All Armed Forces	9/3/1926	10/21/1927		Yangtze Service Medal
		3/1/1930	12/31/1932		
Expeditionary Medals	Marines	11/21/1903	1/18/1904	Abyssinia: Djibouti	Marine Corps Expeditionary Medal

(continued)

Service	Begin Date	End Date	Location	Campaign
Navy	7/30/1890	7/30/1890	Argentina: Buenos Aires	Navy Expeditionary Medal
	8/28/1891	8/30/1891	Chile: Valparaiso	
	12/4/1894	5/16/1895	China: Tiensin	
	3/1/1895	3/18/1895	China: Chefoo	
	10/10/1911	1/19/1914	China: Peiping, Shanghai	
	10/10/1911	1/19/1914	China: American Legation Guard	
	6/1925	8/31/1925	China: Chefoo	
	4/3/1925		China: Wuchow	
	12/1927		China: Canton	
	4/22/1928	5/15/1928	China: Armed Guard duty onboard S.S. Mei Lu, S.S. I'Ping	
	4/15/1929		China: onboard at Ichang	

(continued)

12/12/1937		China: onboard Panay
4/11/1885	5/22/1885	Panama
3/8/1895	3/9/1895	Boca del Toro
11/11/1901	12/4/1901	Panama
4/17/1902	4/19/1902	Boca del Toro
9/18/1902	9/22/1902	Panama
9/23/1902	11/18/1902	Panama and Colon
11/4/1903	2/26/1904	Panama
11/4/1903	1/3/1904	Colon
12/31/1903		Porto Bello
5/28/1912	8/5/1912	Cuba: Guantanamo Bay
1/3/1961	10/23/1962	Cuba
4/1/1903	4/19/1903	Dominican Rep: Santo Domingo City
1/1/1904	2/1/1904	Dominican Rep: Santo Domingo City

Service	Begin Date	End Date	Location	Campaign
	2/25/1904	2/27/1904	Dominican Rep: San Pedro de Macoris	
	8/15/1914	10/30/1914	Dominican Republic	
	11/26/1914	12/11/1914	Dominican Republic	
	10/31/1914	11/14/1914	Haiti	
	12/13/1914	12/17/1914	Haiti	
	12/5/1916	4/5/1917	Dominican Republic	
	11/12/1918	9/1/1924	Dominican Republic	
	6/10/1882	8/29/1882	Egypt: Alexandria	
	5/2/1891	6/20/1891	Haiti: Navassa Island	
	1/26/1914	2/10/1914	Haiti: Port-au-Prince	

(continued)

2/1/1914	2/3/1914	Haiti: Gonaives
10/18/1914	11/7/1914	Haiti: Cape Haitian
12/7/1915	4/5/1917	Haiti
11/12/1918	3/31/1919	Haiti
6/16/1920	11/25/1924	Haiti
12/4/1929	8/5/1931	Haiti
2/12/1874	2/20/1874	Hawaii: Honolulu
7/30/1889	7/31/1889	Hawaii: Honolulu
1/16/1893	4/1/1893	Hawaii: Honolulu
3/21/1903	4/16/1903	Honduras: Truxillo, La Ceiba, Puerto Cortez
4/28/1907	5/23/1907	Honduras: Laguna
5/4/1907	6/8/1907	Honduras: Choloma
2/28/1924	3/13/1924	Honduras: La Ceiba, Puerto Cortez, Tela

Service	Begin Date	End Date	Location	Campaign
	3/18/1924	4/30/1924	Honduras: Tegulcigalpa	
	12/8/1978	6/6/1979	Indian Ocean, Iran, Yemen	
	11/21/1979	10/20/1981	Indian Ocean, Iran	
	6/19/1888	6/30/1888	Korea: Seoul	
	7/24/1894	4/3/1896	Korea: Seoul	
	1/5/1904	11/11/1905	Korea: Am. Legation Guard, Seoul	
	8/20/1982	5/31/1983	Lebanon, Beruit	
	1/20/1986	6/27/1986	Libya	
	8/5/1990	2/21/1991	Liberia	
	7/6/1894	8/7/1894	Nicaragua: Bluefields	
	5/2/1896	5/4/1896	Nicaragua: Corinto	
	2/7/1898	2/8/1898	Nicaragua: San Juan del Sur	

(continued)

2/24/1899	2/28/1899	Nicaragua: Bluefields
12/20/1909	3/15/1910	Nicaragua: Corinto
5/30/1910	9/4/1910	Nicaragua: Bluefields
11/15/1912	4/5/1917	Nicaragua: Legation Guard, Managua
11/12/1918	8/3/1925	Nicaragua: Legation Guard, Managua
5/7/1926	6/4/1926	Nicaragua: Bluefields
9/17/1911	11/18/1911	Philippines
2/1/1987	7/23/1987	Persian Gulf
12/1905	1/1/1907	Russia: Embassy Guard, St. Petersburg
4/7/1994	4/18/1994	Rwanda
11/13/1888	3/20/1889	Samoa: Apia

Service	Begin Date	End Date	Location	Campaign
	3/1899	5/1899	Samoa: Apia	
	3/31/1920	11/19/1922	Siberia: Russian Island	
	9/8/1903	9/13/1903	Syria: Beirut	
	10/10/1903	10/17/1903	Syria: Beirut	
	5/16/1962	8/10/1962	Thailand	
	6/28/1921	7/3/1921	Turkey: Ismir	
	9/8/1922	10/18/1922	Turkey: Smyrna	
	12/7/1941	12/22/1941	Wake Island	
China				
Navy and Marines	7/7/1937	9/7/1939		China Service Medal
Navy and Marines	9/2/1945	4/1/1957	also includes Coast Guard	
Army and Navy	9/8/1939	12/7/1941		American Defense Service Medal
WWII				
Army Women	7/10/1942	8/31/1943	Women's Army Aux. Corps	Women's Army Corps Service Medal

		9/1/1943	9/2/1945	Women's Army Corps	
	All Armed Forces	12/7/1941	3/2/1946	American Theater	American Campaign
	All Armed Forces	12/7/1941	11/8/1945	Europe and Africa	European-African-Middle Eastern Campaign Medal
	All Armed Forces	12/7/1941	3/2/1946		Asiatic-Pacific Campaign Medal
	All Armed Forces	12/7/1941	12/31/1946		WWII Victory Medal
Occupation Medals					
	Army and Air Force	5/9/1945	5/5/1955	Germany	Army of Occupation Medal
		5/9/1945	7/27/1955	Austria	
		5/9/1945	10/2/1990	Berlin	
		5/9/1945	9/15/1947	Italy	
		9/3/1945	4/27/1952	Japan	
		9/3/1945	6/29/1949	Korea	
	Navy and Marines	5/8/1945	5/5/1955	Germany	Navy Occupation Service Medal

(continued)

	Service	Begin Date	End Date	Location	Campaign
		5/8/1945	12/15/1947	Italy	
		5/8/1945	10/25/1955	Trieste	
		5/8/1945	10/25/1955	Austria	
		5/8/1945	10/2/1990	Berlin	
		9/2/1945	4/27/1952	Japan	
		9/2/1945	4/27/1952	Korea	
Berlin Airlift	All Forces	6/23/1948	5/12/1949		Medal for Humane Action
Korea	All Forces	6/27/1950	7/27/1954		Korean Service Medal
National Defense Service	All Forces	6/27/1950	7/27/1954		National Defense Service Medal
		1/1/1961	8/14/1974		
		8/2/1990	11/30/1995		
		9/11/2001	continued		

Expeditionary Medals

All Forces		
7/1/1958	11/1/1958	Lebanon

Armed Forces Expeditionary Medal		
7/1/1958	7/3/1965	Vietnam
8/23/1958	6/1965	Quemoy and Matsu Islands
8/23/1958	1/1959	Taiwan Straits
7/14/1960	9/1/1962	Congo
4/19/1961	10/7/1962	Laos
8/14/1961	6/1/1963	Berlin
10/24/1962	6/1/1963	Cuba
11/23/1964	11/27/1964	Congo
4/28/1965	9/28/1966	Dominican Republic
10/1/1966	6/30/1974	Korea
3/29/1973	8/15/1973	Cambodia
3/29/1973	8/15/1973	Thailand
4/11/1975	4/13/1975	Cambodia
4/29/1975	4/30/1975	Vietnam
5/15/1975		Mayaguez Operation

(continued)

Service	Begin Date	End Date	Location	Campaign
	1/1/1981	2/1/1992	El Salvador	
	6/1/1983	12/1/1987	Lebanon	
	10/23/1983	11/21/1983	Grenada	
	4/12/1986	4/17/1986	Libya	
	7/24/1987	8/1/1990	Persian Gulf	
	12/20/1989	1/31/1990	Panama	
	12/5/1992	3/31/1995	Somalia	
	9/16/1994	3/31/1995	Haiti	
	12/1/1995	12/31/1996	Turkey and Northern Iraq	
	6/1/1992	12/19/1996	Bosnia	
	6/1/1992	12/20/1995	Bosnia	
	12/20/1996	6/20/1998	Bosnia	
	6/21/1998	12/31/2000	Bosnia	
	12/1/1995	cont.	Southwest Asia: Op. Southern Watch	
	1/1/1997	cont.	Southwest Asia: Op. Northern Watch	

	12/1/1995	9/1/1997	Southwest Asia: Op. Vigilant Sentinel
	11/11/1998	12/22/1998	Southwest Asia: Op. Desert Thunder
	12/16/1998	12/22/1998	Southwest Asia: Op. Desert Fox
	12/31/1998	12/31/2002	Southwest Asia: Op. Desert Springs
	12/1/1995	cont.	Southwest Asia: Op. Maritime Intercept
	3/24/1999	5/3/2000	Kosovo
Vietnam	All Forces 7/3/1965	3/28/1973	Vietnam Service Medal — includes Thailand, Laos and Cambodia

(continued)

Service	Begin Date	End Date	Location	Campaign
Saudi Arabia, Kuwait				
All Forces	8/2/1990	1/16/1991	Saudi Arabia	Southwest Asia Service Medal
	1/17/1992	4/11/1992	Kuwait ceasefire	
	4/12/1992	11/30/1995		
Kosovo				
All Forces	3/24/1999	TBD		Kosovo Campaign Medal
Global War on Terror, Afghan., Iraq				
All Forces	9/11/2001	continued	Afghanistan	Global War on Terrorism Expeditionary Medal
	9/11/2001	continued	Iraq	
Korea				
All Forces	7/28/1954	continued	Korea	Korean Defense Service Medal

ACKNOWLEDGMENTS

THIS BOOK HAD ITS ORIGINS in a bar in Durham, North Carolina. I was in town in December 2008 to present a paper, and I had drinks with my friend, the constitutional scholar H. Jefferson Powell. When I mentioned that I was writing an essay about the idea of wartime, Jeff interrupted, and insisted that the essay had to be a book, and I had to write it immediately. And so a larger study of the impact of war on American democracy during the twentieth century turned into two books, beginning with this one.

The discussion over drinks in Durham was just one of a number of conversations with extraordinary people that has helped produce this volume. Brilliant works by Marilyn Young on endless war, and by Carol Greenhouse and Lynn Hunt on time were guiding lights. I have benefited greatly from everyone who read a paper, came to talk, asked a question, offered an argument, sent an e-mail, and even posted a blog comment. More than anything else I have written, these ideas developed through my conversations with you.

This work would not be possible without generous support from a number of institutions. I began my broader, ongoing project on war and democracy in twentieth-century America while a member of the School of Social Science, Institute for Advanced Study, Princeton, in 2007–08, and also with the support of a John Simon Guggenheim Foundation Fellowship. The University of Southern California provided important research funding in the form of an Advancing Scholarship in the Humanities and Social Sciences Research Grant. Thanks to Robert Rasmussen, dean of USC Gould School of Law, for support including a crucial semester's leave to finish the writing, and to former interim dean Edward McCaffery.

I am grateful to the deans, faculty, and graduate and law students at these institutions where I was invited to speak, and I regret that I cannot name each person who has had an influence: School of Social Science, Institute for Advanced Study, Princeton; Centre for American Studies, University of Leicester; Tainament Library Cold War Seminar, NYU; Hauser Colloquium, NYU Law School; Warren Center for American History and Kennedy School of Government, Harvard University; Boston College Law School; University of Chicago Law School; University of Connecticut Law School; Duke Law School; University of Minnesota Law School; Ohio Legal History Workshop, Ohio State University; USC Gould School of Law; University of Texas Law School; Vanderbilt Law School; University of Virginia Law School; Santa Clara Law School; U.C. Davis Law School; University of Oregon; Departments of History at USC, UCLA, and Fordham University; panels at the Cold War Cultures Conference, University of Texas; and American Society for Legal History Annual Meeting.

I thank commentators and careful readers of various papers for their criticism and insight, including Danielle Allen, Thomas Allen, Robert Chesney, Dennis Hutchinson, Robert Keohane, Allison LaCroix, Michael Shapiro, Mark Tushnet, and Steven Wilf. Special thanks to Dirk Bonker, Lynn Hunt, Lary May, Marita Sturken, and Marilyn Young for comments on an earlier draft of the book and to Jeffrey Dunoff, Peter Spiro, and participants in a Roundtable on the book, sponsored by the Institute for International Law and Public Policy, Temple Law School.

Pulling the threads of this work together required me to read across many literatures. I could only accomplish this with the expert help of what seemed like legions of librarians. Marcia Tucker at the History and Social Sciences Library, Institute for Advanced Study, helped me get started. No thank-you can be sufficient for all the work librarians at USC Gould School of Law devoted to this project, including Luis Alas, Cindy Guyer, Diana Jaques, Rosanne Krikorian, Paul Moorman, Anahit Petrosyan, Brian Raphael, Claudia Raphael, and others. The Lompoc Valley Historical Society provided crucial help, as did archivists at the National Archives. My research assistants have also been indispensable: Matthew Crossman, Nicole Giuntoli, Allison Lauterberg, Christina Lee, Kyle Montes de Oca, Sam Perry, Habeeb Syed, and Oberlin College students Alicia Dudziak and Vera Tykulsker. Susan Davis made sure I had what I needed no matter where on the planet I happened to be. Thanks to my editor at Oxford University Press, Tim Bent, who gave the manuscript careful attention, to Joellyn Ausanka for shepherding it along, and to my careful yet merciful copy editor, Sylvia Cannizzaro. Thanks also to Sandy Dijkstra, my literary agent, for her support.

My most heartfelt thanks are to my family. William Aitkenhead Sr. lent me his medals from World War II and after, while Elizabeth Aitkenhead asked important questions. My husband, Bill Aitkenhead, and my daughter, Alicia Dudziak, turned the book into a family project and tolerated my need to turn the entire house into a somewhat disheveled library. Alicia has been a great editor, proofreader, and occasional researcher. Bill found time for this book in his own busy life, and helped me see where I needed to be clearer. He manages the details of everyday life when I have a deadline, and he reads every word, over and over, certainly the greatest gift a writer could hope for.

NOTES

Introduction

1. Eric J. Leed, *No Man's Land: Conflict and Identity in World War I* (Cambridge: Cambridge University Press, 1979), 129; Stephen Kern, *The Culture of Time and Space, 1880–1918*, 2nd ed. (Cambridge, MA: Harvard University Press, 2003), 288–312.
2. Cheryl A. Wells, *Civil War Time: Temporality and Identity in America, 1861–1865* (Atlanta: University of Georgia Press, 2005), 1.
3. Saby Ghoshray, "When Does Collateral Damage Rise to the Level of a War Crime? Expanding the Adequacy of Laws of War against Contemporary Human Rights Discourse," *Creighton Law Review* 41, no. 4 (2008): 679–711, 687.
4. Giorgio Agamben, *State of Exception*, trans. Kevin Attell (Chicago: University of Chicago Press, 2005), 4; Lee Epstein, Daniel E. Ho, Gary King, and Jeffrey A. Segal, "The Supreme Court during Crisis: How War Affects Only Non-War Cases," *New York University Law Review* 80 (April 2005): 1–116 (citing the literature on courts and wartime).

5. On the way Pearl Harbor is remembered, see Emily S. Rosenberg, *A Date Which Will Live: Pearl Harbor in American Memory* (Durham, NC: Duke University Press, 2003).
6. Barack Obama, "Remarks by the President in Address to the Nation on the End of Combat Operations in Iraq," August 31, 2010, http://www.whitehouse.gov/the-press-office/2010/08/31/remarks-president-address-nation-end-combat-operations-iraq.

Chapter 1

1. "Today a Clock Is Man's Best Friend," February 9, 1942, *Cleveland Plain Dealer*, 1, 3. I am grateful to Alicia Dudziak and Vera Tykulsker for research help with the *Cleveland Plain Dealer*.
2. Michael O'Malley, *Keeping Watch: A History of American Time* (New York: Penguin, 1990), 23–98; David Prerau, *Seize the Daylight: The Curious and Contentious Story of Daylight Saving Time* (New York: Basic Books, 2005); Michael Downing, *Spring Forward: The Annual Madness of Daylight Saving Time*, rev. ed. (Berkeley, CA: Counterpoint, 2007).
3. Statement of Hon. Donald H. McLean, A Representative in Congress from the State of New Jersey, Hearings before a Subcommittee of the Committee on Interstate and Foreign Commerce, House of Representatives, on H.R. 5343: A Bill to Promote the National Defense and the Conservation of Electrical Energy by Permitting the Establishment of Daylight-Saving Time (also on H.R. 3789, H.R. 4206, H.R. 4522, H.R. 5088, H.R. 5219), 77th Cong., 1st sess., Aug. 7, 1941, pp. 84, 90, 94; Statement of A. Julian Brylawski, Vice President of the Motion Picture Theater Owners of America, Hearings before a Subcommittee of the Committee on Interstate and Foreign Commerce, House of Representatives, on H.R. 5343: A Bill to Promote the National Defense and the Conservation of Electrical Energy by Permitting the Establishment of Daylight-Saving Time (also on H.R. 3789, H.R. 4206, H.R. 4522, H.R. 5088, H.R. 5219), 77th Cong., 1st sess., Aug. 7, 1941, p. 109.

4. Statement of Hon. Eugene J. Keogh, A Representative in Congress from the State of New York, Hearings before a Subcommittee of the Committee on Interstate and Foreign Commerce, House of Representatives, on H.R. 5343: A Bill to Promote the National Defense and the Conservation of Electrical Energy by Permitting the Establishment of Daylight-Saving Time (also on H.R. 3789, H.R. 4206, H.R. 4522, H.R. 5088, H.R. 5219), 77th Cong., 1st sess., Aug. 5, 1941, pp. 4–5; Statement of Leland Olds, Chairman, Federal Power Commission, Hearings before a Subcommittee of the Committee on Interstate and Foreign Commerce, House of Representatives, on H.R. 5343: A Bill to Promote the National Defense and the Conservation of Electrical Energy by Permitting the Establishment of Daylight-Saving Time (also on H.R. 3789, H.R. 4206, H.R. 4522, H.R. 5088, H.R. 5219), 77th Cong., 1st sess., Aug. 5, 1941, pp. 6–10.

5. Statement of Leland Olds, 11–19, 27.

6. Oklahoma State Senate, Senate Resolution No. 2, reprinted in Hearings before a Subcommittee of the Committee on Interstate and Foreign Commerce, House of Representatives, on H.R. 875, 4489; Testimony of Hugh F. Hall, American Farm Bureau Federation, Hearings before a Subcommittee of the Committee on Interstate and Foreign Commerce, House of Representatives, on H.R. 875, 4489; H. Con. Res. 81, 10, 9; and H.R. 3829, Time: Pacific, Daylight Saving, and Standard, 78th Cong., 2nd Sess., Nov. 9, 1943, May 11 and 12, 1944, pp. 7–8, 13, 28.

7. Statement of Lt. Col. Theron D. Weaver, Office of the Under Secretary of War, Hearings before a Subcommittee of the Committee on Interstate and Foreign Commerce, House of Representatives, on H.R. 5343: A Bill to Promote the National Defense and the Conservation of Electrical Energy by Permitting the Establishment of Daylight-Saving Time (also on H.R. 3789, H.R. 4206, H.R. 4522, H.R. 5088, H.R. 5219), 77th Cong., 1st sess., Aug. 6, 1941, p. 80.

8. "Street Lights to Go on War Time," February 7, 1942, *Cleveland Plain Dealer*, 13. On the way Americans acclimated to government power during World War II, see James T. Sparrow, *Warfare State: World War II Americans and the Age of Big Government* (New York: Oxford University Press, 2011).

9. Emily Rosenberg, *A Date Which Will Live: Pearl Harbor and American Memory* (Durham, NC: Duke University Press, 2003); Cheryl A. Wells, *Civil War Time: Temporality and Identity in America, 1861–1865* (Atlanta: University of Georgia Press, 2005), 1. The Civil War, however, did not fully replace concepts of time held by nineteenth-century Americans. Instead, Wells suggests that overlapping ideas about time, based on the clock, religion, the seasons, and the sun and moon, were held in the South and North before the war and after. The war interceded with its own "battle time," which "reconfigured antebellum temporalities." War was carried on in a complex "temporal web," as "booming cannons superseded watches' and clocks' ability to order society, and God's time became increasingly secular in the face of battle." Beyond the battlefield, many had to "abandon the modernity of the clock and embrace, at least during the war, task orientation." Wells, *Civil War Time*, 5. On the way the Civil War has been remembered, see David W. Blight, *Race and Reunion: The Civil War in American Memory* (Cambridge, MA: Belknap Press, 2001); Alice Fahs and Joan Waugh, eds., *The Memory of the Civil War in American Culture* (Chapel Hill: University of North Carolina Press, 2004).

On the idea of post–World War II as "postwar," Tony Judt's epic work on Europe after World War II is simply titled *Postwar: A History of Europe since 1945* (New York: Penguin, 2005). Continuous U.S. engagement in war since 1945 is discussed in many works including Adrian R. Lewis, *The American Culture of War: The History of U.S. Military Force from World War II to Operation Iraqi Freedom* (New York: Routledge, 2007).

10. See, e.g., William Rehnquist, *All the Laws But One: Civil Liberties in Wartime* (New York: Knopf, 1998), 218–25; Geoffrey

R. Stone, *Perilous Times: Free Speech in Wartime from the Sedition Act of 1798 to the War on Terrorism* (New York: Norton, 2004), 12–13, 527–30, 535–55.

11. The phrase *Inter arma silent leges*, originally *Silent enim leges inter arma*, is attributed to Cicero. See Fred R. Shapiro, ed., *The Yale Book of Quotations* (New Haven, CT: Yale University Press, 2006), 156. According to Saby Ghoshrav, "[s]ome of the more notable usages of the term have been found in a few Supreme Court decisions" including Justice Antonin Scalia's opinion in *Hamdi v. Rumsfeld*, 542 U.S. 507, 569 (2004). Saby Ghoshray, "When Does Collateral Damage Rise to the Level of a War Crime: Expanding the Adequacy of Laws of War against Contemporary Human Rights Discourse," *Creighton Law Review* 41, no. 4 (2008): 687.

On civil liberties and wartime, see, e.g., Louis Fisher, *The Constitution and 9/11: Recurring Threats to America's Freedoms* (Lawrence: University Press of Kansas, 2008) xii–xvi; Michael Linfield, *Freedom under Fire: U.S. Civil Liberties in Times of War* (Boston: South End Press, 1990), 5–7; Shira A. Scheindlin and Matthew L. Schwartz, "With All Due Deference: Judicial Responsibility in a Time of Crisis," *Hofstra Law Review* 32 (Spring 2004): 795–852; Zechariah Chafee Jr., "Freedom of Speech in Wartime," *Harvard Law Review* 32, no. 8 (1919): 932–43. See also Lee Epstein, Daniel E. Ho, Gary King, and Jeffrey A. Segal, "The Supreme Court during Crisis: How War Affects Only Non-War Cases," *New York University Law Review* 80 (April 2005): 5–9, 18–20 (citing adherents to the "crisis thesis").

Many scholars decry the idea that law applies differently during war, but nevertheless tend to view the courts as acting differently during wartime. See Oren Gross and Fionnuala Ní Aoláin, *Law in Times of Crisis: Emergency Powers in Theory and Practice* (Cambridge: Cambridge University Press, 2006), 98–105; Epstein, Ho, King, and Segal, "Supreme Court during Crisis," 1, 5–9, 18–20 (citing examples). The contrary example of the Supreme Court protecting rights and limiting executive power during war is the Civil War–era case *Ex Parte Milligan*, 71 U.S. 2 (1866), which Clinton Rossiter calls "the great exception." Clinton

Rossiter, *The Supreme Court and the Commander in Chief*, rev. ed. (Ithaca, NY: Cornell University Press, 1976), 26–39.

12. George W. Bush, "President Bush Announces Major Combat Operations in Iraq Have Ended," May 1, 2003, http://georgewbush-whitehouse.archives.gov/news/releases/2003/05/20030501-15.html; Barack Obama, "Remarks by the President in Address to the Nation on the End of Combat Operations in Iraq," August 31, 2010, http://www.whitehouse.gov/the-press-office/2010/08/31/remarks-president-address-nation-end-combat-operations-iraq.

13. Lynn Hunt, *Measuring Time, Making History* (Budapest: Central European University Press, 2008), 4–5. See also William H. Sewell Jr., *Logics of History: Social Theory and Social Transformation* (Chicago: University of Chicago Press, 2005), 11. There is a body of work on the history of time-keeping. See, e.g., David S. Landes, *Revolution in Time: Clocks and the Making of the Modern World*, rev. ed. (Cambridge, MA: Belknap Press, 2000). Scholarship on time in U.S. history expands on E. P. Thompson's classic work, "Time, Work-Discipline, and Industrial Capitalism," *Past and Present* 38 (Dec. 1967): 56–97, finding the impact of mechanical time beyond the factory, and exploring other ways that time is framed and divided. For example, Mark Smith explores the impact of clock-time on Southern slavery in *Mastered by the Clock: Time, Slavery, and Freedom in the American South* (Chapel Hill: University of North Carolina Press, 1997). Alexis McCrossen focuses on the cultural meanings of "Sunday" in *Holy Day, Holiday: The American Sunday* (Ithaca, NY: Cornell University Press, 2000).

14. Emile Durkheim, *Elementary Forms of Religious Life*, trans. J. W. Swain, 2nd ed. (New York: Free Press, 1976), 10; Carol J. Greenhouse, *A Moment's Notice: Time Politics across Cultures* (Ithaca, NY: Cornell University Press, 1996), 26–27.

15. Greenhouse, *A Moment's Notice*, 19–28.

16. Ibid., 19–28, 183–84.

17. Ibid., 23. An example of cyclical time is the ordering of farm chores according to the seasons in Robert D. Thomas, *The Old Farmer's Almanac* (Dublin, NH: Yankee Publishing, 2008). One cultural use of linear time appears in American law. According to Greenhouse, law involves "the constant expansion of a linear time framework in the production and use of 'precedent.'" Law's endpoint in this linear progression, however, "is neither fixed nor envisioned. It is symbolically coterminous with national social life." Greenhouse, *A Moment's Notice*, 184. Law's temporality is distinctive, she argues, both because it is cumulative ("*all* interests and histories can be represented as pertaining to the social field in which the law operates"), and because it is reversible (past decisions can control present ones; and precedent can be reversed). Greenhouse, *A Moment's Notice*, 184.

18. Thompson, "Time, Work-Discipline, and Industrial Capitalism," 56; David Brody, "Time and Work during Early American Industrialization," *Labor and History* 30 (Winter 1989): 5–46; Gerhard Dohrn-van Rossum, *History of the Hour: Clocks and Modern Temporal Orders*, trans. Thomas Dunlap (Chicago: University of Chicago Press, 1996), 289–323, 347–50; Stephen Kern, *The Culture of Time and Space, 1880–1918*, 2nd ed. (Cambridge, MA: Harvard University Press, 2003), 11–15; Wells, *Civil War Time*, 7; Smith, *Mastered by the Clock*, 178–84; Landes, *Revolution in Time*, 303–4; Eviatar Zerubavel, "The Standardization of Time: A Sociohistorical Perspective," *American Journal of Sociology* 88 (July 1982): 1–23; Benedict Anderson, *Imagined Communities: Reflections on the Origin and Spread of Nationalism*, rev. ed. (London: Verso, 2006), 24–26; Thomas M. Allen, *A Republic in Time: Temporality and Social Imagination in Nineteenth-Century America* (Chapel Hill: University of North Carolina Press, 2008), 6.

19. Allen, *Republic in Time*, 10–11; Greenhouse, *A Moment's Notice*, 1–4. Allen argues that there is a need for new scholarship on the relationship between time and the nation that "attend[s] to the recursive and dynamic interactions between these two terms."

The historian William Sewell argues that historians embrace the idea of differences in time, even if they don't confront it directly. Historians "have implicit or working theories about social temporality." They tend to "believe that time is *fateful*. Time is irreversible in the sense that an action, once taken, or an event, once experienced, cannot be obliterated. It is lodged in the memory of those whom it affects and therefore irrevocably alters the situation in which it occurs." Further, historians believe that "every act is part of a *sequence* of actions and that its effects are profoundly dependent upon its place in the sequence . . . historians assume that the outcome of any action, event, or trend is likely to be *contingent*, that its effects will depend upon the particular complex temporal sequence of which it is a part." Within this framework, Sewell argues, ideas about time shared by historians are complex, embracing a "diversity of temporalities" and seeing different historical eras as having "different rates of change." This "temporal homogeneity implies *causal heterogeneity*. It implies that the consequences of a given act are not intrinsic in the act but rather will depend on the nature of the social world within which it takes place." Sewell, *Logics of History*, 6–7, 9–10.

Sewell identifies teleological forms of temporality in some works. For Karl Marx, Emile Durkheim, and others, Sewell suggests, history was viewed as "the temporal working out of an inherent logic of social development. . . . The direction and meaning of history were a consequence not of the largely contingent events that made up the surface of history but of long-term, anonymous causal forces, of which particular historical events were at best manifestations." Some works in legal history are consistent with teleological conceptions of time. Finding an inherent progress narrative in legal history, or viewing the path of the law as one of modernization, involves teleological conceptions of temporality, in which the fundamental direction of legal change is driven by larger forces outside the particularities of the experience and acts of those who encounter the law. Sewell, *Logics of History*, 83–84. On progress narratives in legal history, see Mary L. Dudziak, "*Brown* and the Idea of Progress in American Legal History: A Comment on

William Nelson," *St. Louis University Law Journal* 48 (Spring 2004): 851–58.

20. On public and private times, see Kern, *The Culture of Time and Space*, 33–34, 288.

21. Randolph S. Bourne, "The State," in *War and the Intellectuals: Collected Essays, 1915–1919* (New York: Harper & Row, 1964), 65.

22. Kern discusses the idea of the future in *The Culture of Time and Space*, 89–108.

23. Hunt, *Measuring Time, Making History*, 70–71 (quoting Barére); Leo Gershoy, *Bertrand Barère: A Reluctant Terrorist* (Princeton, NJ: Princeton University Press, 1962) 175, 186–87, 231; Leo Gershoy, "Barère , Champion of Nationalism in the French Revolution," *Political Science Quarterly* 3 (September 1927): 424–27.

24. Gross and Aoláin, *Law in Times of Crisis*, 179. See also Matthew Craven, Malgosia Fitzmaurice, and Maria Vogiatzi, eds., *Time, History, and International Law* (Leiden: Nijhoff, 2006); Geoffrey R. Stone, *Perilous Times: Free Speech in Wartime* (New York: Norton, 2004), 5 (emphasis in original). Other writers, including Supreme Court Chief Justice William Rehnquist, also focus on times of war as a way to discern lessons for the future.In *All the Laws but One*, Rehnquist focuses thirteen of his eighteen chapters on the Civil War. Since Rehnquist, like Stone, intends to draw lessons from history for contemporary law, the very structure of the book makes clear that, for him, the Civil War provided the most significant lessons. The Civil War was followed by a long stretch of peacetime, "briefly interrupted in 1898 by the Spanish-American war," but that conflict "lasted only a few months, and it was sufficiently short and one-sided as to pose little danger to civil liberties," he writes. In the remaining chapters, Rehnquist discusses civil liberties during World War I and World War II. The book's scope is limited to declared wars, Rehnquist writes, because "the government's authority to engage in conduct that infringes civil liberty is greatest in time of declared war." Rehnquist, *All the Laws but One*, 171. See also Thomas I. Emerson, *A*

System of Freedom of Expression (New York: Random House, 1970), 55–56; Mark Tushnet, "Defending *Korematsu:* Reflections on Civil Liberties in Wartime," *Wisconsin Law Review* 2003, no. 2 (2003): 273–308.

Stone's chapters also track wartimes, though chapter 1 is a bit ambiguous, focusing on "the 'Half War' with France" in the late eighteenth and early nineteenth centuries. Remaining chapters follow the trajectory of iconic American wartimes: the Civil War, World War I, World War II, the Cold War, and Vietnam. Stone, *Perilous Times*, 5.

On other forms of temporality in legal history, see Christopher Tomlins, "Revolutionary Justice in Brecht, Conrad, and Blake," *Law and Literature* 21, no. 2 (Summer 2009): 185–213; Alison LaCroix, "Temporal Imperialism," *University of Pennsylvania Law Review* 158 (April 2010): 1329–73; Steven Wilf, *The Law before the Law* (Plymouth, UK: Lexington Books, 2008).

25. *Schenck v. United States*, 249 U.S. 47, 48–53 (1919); Espionage Act of 1917 § 3, 64 Pub. L. 24, ch. 30, 44 stat. 217, 219 (1917); Stone, *Perilous Times*, 146–60, 184–96, 198–211. *See also* Paul L. Murphy, *World War I and the Origin of Civil Liberties in the United States* (New York: Norton, 1980).

26. Stone, *Perilous Times*, 185; Sedition Act of 1918, Public Law 65–150, 65th Cong., 2d sess. (40 Stat. 553, 553) (1918); *Abrams v. United States*, 250 U.S. 616, 627–28 (1919). In providing the occasion for Holmes to articulate a more robust First Amendment vision, perhaps war both restricted rights and laid the basis for their later expansion. Mark Tushnet makes a similar argument about *Korematsu* in an essay "Defending *Korematsu?* Reflections on Civil Liberties in Wartime," in *The Constitution in Wartime: Beyond Alarmism and Complacency*, ed. Mark Tushnet (Durham, NC: Duke University Press, 2005), 124–40. Compared to the traditional image of a pendulum swinging from protection of rights in peacetime to security in wartime, the development of a more robust rights jurisprudence in reaction to war suggests that a more complicated image is required.

27. Stone, *Perilous Times*, 535; Todd Gitlin, *The Whole World Is Watching: Mass Media in the Making and Unmaking of the New Left* (Los Angeles: University of California Press, 1980), 6. On the importance of frames to our understanding of the world we occupy, see Erving Goffman, *Frame Analysis: An Essay on the Organization of Experience* (New York: Harper & Row, 1974).

28. Stone, *Perilous Times*, 5. In contrast to Stone, some scholars view the impact of war as continuous rather than episodic, and Mark Brandon comes to the opposite calculation about the extent of wartime versus peacetime, finding that military engagement has occurred through "80 percent of the life of the nation." Mark Brandon, "War and the American Constitutional Order," in Tushnet, *The Constitution in Wartime*, 11. On small wars in the twentieth century, see, e.g., Max Boot, *The Savage Wars of Peace: Small Wars and the Rise of American Power* (New York: Basic Books, 2002); Mary Renda, *Taking Haiti: Military Occupation and the Culture of U.S. Imperialism* (Chapel Hill: University of North Carolina Press, 2001); Paul A. Kramer, *The Blood of Government: Race, Empire, the United States, and the Philippines* (Chapel Hill: University of North Carolina Press, 2006).

29. Francis Wormuth and Edwin Brown Firmage, *To Chain the Dog of War: The War Power of Congress in History and Law*, 2nd ed. (Urbana-Champaign: University of Illinois Press, 1989); Gary Hess, *Presidential Decisions for War: Korea, Vietnam, and the Persian Gulf* (Baltimore: Johns Hopkins University Press, 2001); George C. Herring, *America's Longest War: The United States and Vietnam, 1950–1975*, 2nd ed. (Philadelphia: Temple University Press, 1986). On congressional ratification of post-9/11 military action, see, e.g., Curtis A. Bradley and Jack L. Goldsmith, "Congressional Authorization and the War on Terrorism," *Harvard Law Review* 118 (May 2005): 2047–2133; Ryan Goodman and Derek Jinks, "International Law, U.S. War Powers, and the Global War on Terrorism," *Harvard Law Review* 118 (June 2005): 2653–62.

30. "Wartime," in *The Oxford Essential Dictionary of the U.S. Military* (New York: Oxford University Press, 2001); *Prize Cases*, 67 U.S. 635, 666 (1863); John Whiteclay Chambers II, ed., *The Oxford Companion to American Military History* (New York: Oxford University Press, 2000), 773–75; Hedley Bull, *The Anarchical Society: A Study of Order in World Politics*, 3rd ed. (New York: Columbia University Press, 2002), 178–179.

31. Elaine Tyler May, "Echoes of the Cold War: The Aftermath of September 11," in *September 11 in History: A Watershed Moment?* ed. Mary L. Dudziak (Durham, NC: Duke University Press, 2003), 38–40. On the history of U.S. airpower and the way it has been imagined, see Michael S. Sherry, *The Rise of American Air Power: The Creation of Armageddon* (New Haven, CT: Yale University Press, 1987).

32. John E. Strandberg and Roger James Bender, *"The Call of Duty": Military Awards and Decorations of the United States of America*, 2nd ed. (San Jose, CA: Bender, 2004), 247; Brent C. Bankus, "We've Done This Before," *Small Wars Journal* 4 (February 2006): 33–36.

33. Thomas A. Richards, "Foreword," in Fred L. Borch and Charles P. McDowell, *Sea Service Medals: Military Awards and Decorations of the Navy, Marine Corps, and Coast Guard* (Annapolis, MD: Naval Institute Press, 2009), ix; Strandberg and Bender, *The Call of Duty*, 248.

34. Keith B. Bickel, *Mars Learning: The Marine Corps' Development of Small Wars Doctrine, 1915–1940* (Boulder, CO: Westview, 2001), 1, quoting United States Marine Corps, *Small Wars Manual* (Quantico, VA: Marine Corps Schools, 1940; reprint, Manhattan, KS: Sunflower University Press, 1987), 1; Strandberg and Bender, *The Call of Duty*, 294–99.

35. "VFW Eligibility Information," October 2005, Veterans of Foreign Wars, http://www.vfw.org/resources/pdf/eligibility05.pdf; Disabled American Veterans, Constitution and ByLaws, 2, 54–55, http://www.dav.org/membership/documents/ConstitutionBylaws.pdf; The American Legion, http://www.legion.org/join. While the American Legion begins World War II with Pearl Harbor, the Disabled American

Veterans counts a previous year, September 16, 1940, to December 7, 1941, as service under "conditions simulating war," qualifying disabled veterans for membership. Paralyzed Veterans of America is more inclusive than other organizations, opening membership to all veterans of the U.S. Armed forces with spinal cord injuries, except those with dishonorable discharges. Paralyzed Veterans of America, http:// www.pva.org/site/PageServer?pagename=memb_eligibility.

36. Byron Farwell, *Queen Victoria's Little Wars* (New York: Norton, 1985); Martti Koskenniemi, *The Gentle Civilizer of Nations: The Rise and Fall of International Law 1870–1960* (Cambridge: Cambridge University Press, 2004); Paul A. Kramer, *The Blood of Government: Race, Empire, the United States, and the Philippines* (Chapel Hill: University of North Carolina Press, 2006).

37. Greg Grandin, *Empire's Workshop: Latin America, the United States, and the Rise of the New Imperialism* (New York: Holt, 2006), 2, 23.

38. Amy Kaplan, "Where Is Guantánamo?" in *Legal Borderlands: Law and the Construction of American Borders*, ed. Mary L. Dudziak and Leti Volpp (Baltimore: Johns Hopkins University Press, 2006), 240.

Chapter 2

1. "Four Sentenced to Die in Camp Cooke Murder," *Los Angeles Times*, September 15, 1949, 1; *Lee v. Madigan*, 248 F.2d 783 (9th Cir. 1957); *Lee v. Madigan*, 358 U.S. 228, 229–30 (1959); Article of War 92, 10 U.S.C. § 1564 (1946); Opinion of the Board of Review, United States v. William D. Barnes, Clarence Coons, John Lee, and Richard Spasoff, Department of the Army, Office of the Judge Advocate General, March 29, 1950, p. 2; Articles of War, 10 U.S.C. § 1564 (Supp. IV 1951)(Article 92).

The leading work on Cold War–era courts-martial is Elizabeth Lutes Hillman, *Defending America: Military Culture and the Cold War Court-Martial* (Princeton, NJ: Princeton University Press, 2005). See also Jonathan Lurie, *Military*

Justice in America: The U.S. Court of Appeals for the Armed Forces, 1775–1980 (Lawrence: University Press of Kansas, 2001).

Thanks to Karen Paaske and others at the Lompoc Valley Historical Society, and to the USC Law Library staff for help with research on *Lee v. Madigan* and Camp Cooke.

2. Opinion of the Board of Review, United States v. William D. Barnes, Clarence Coons, John Lee, and Richard Spasoff, Department of the Army, Office of the Judge Advocate General, March 29, 1950; "Paris Gunplay: Three GI Jailbreakers Are Caught after Wild Chase in the Streets," *Life*, May 13, 1946, 117–20.

3. Office of the Historian, Headquarters Twentieth Air Force, "History of Vandenberg Air Force Base: From Cooke to Vandenberg," n.d., 4–5; Averam B. Bender, "From Tanks to Missiles: Camp Cooke/Cooke Air Force Base (California) 1941–1958," *Arizona and the West*, 9 (Autumn 1967): 219–42, 225–26; Jeffrey Geiger, "Historic Posts, Camps, Stations and Airfields: Camp Cooke," The California State Military Museum, http://www.militarymuseum.org/CpCooke.html; "From Rocks to Rockets: A Look at the History of Vandenberg," program at Lompoc Public Library, April 9, 2005, DVD.

4. Deke Houlgate Jr., "Drop in Crime Brings End to Army Prison at Lompoc," *Los Angeles Times*, July 20, 1959, 1, 30; Opinion of the Board of Review, United States v. William D. Barnes, Clarence Coons, John Lee, and Richard Spasoff, p. 8; "Negro Prisoner Killed in D.B.," *Lompoc Record*, June 16, 1949.

5. Opinion of the Board of Review, United States v. William D. Barnes, Clarence Coons, John Lee, and Richard Spasoff, p. 18.

6. *Hamilton v. McClaughry*, 136 F. 445, 446–47, 551 (D. Kan. 1905); Boot, *The Savage Wars of Peace*, 97–98, 336–37; Eileen P. Scully, *Bargaining with the State from Afar: American Citizenship in Treaty Port China, 1844–1942* (New York: Columbia University Press, 2001).

7. *Ex parte Johnson* F.2d 705 (D. Kan. 1925); *United States v. Ayers*, 4 C.M.A. 220, (1954); *United States v. Anderson*, 17

C.M.A. 588 (1968); Uniform Code of Military Justice, U.S. Code 10 (2006), §885; Joseph Romero, "Of War and Punishment: 'Time of War' in Military Jurisprudence and a Call for Congress to Define Its Meaning," *Naval Law Review* 51 (2005): 1–52.

8. "Statement by the President on the Termination of the State of War with Japan," April 28, 1952, *1952–1953 Public Papers*, 302; "Cessation of Hostilities of World War II," December 31, 1946, *1946 Public Papers*, 514; President Harry S. Truman, "President's Proclamation," *New York Times*, January 1, 1947; "Letter to the President of the Senate Recommending Legislation to Terminate the State of War with Germany," July 9, 1951, *1951 Public Papers*, 378; John W. Dower, *Embracing Defeat: Japan in the Wake of World War II* (New York: Norton, 1999), 552–53. See also David M. Kennedy, *Freedom from Fear: The American People in Depression and War, 1929–1945* (New York: Oxford University Press, 1999), 798–851 (dating the end of World War II in 1945).

9. Articles of War, 10 U.S.C. § 1564 (Supp. IV 1951) (Article 92); *Ludecke v. Watkins*, 335 U.S. 160, 169–170 (1948), citing *United States v. Anderson*, 9 Wall. 56, 70.

10. H. R. Rep. No. 2682, 79th Cong., 2d Sess. (1947); H. R. Rep. No. 799, 80th Cong., 1st Sess. (1947); S. Rep. No. 339, 80th Cong., 1st Sess. (1947); *Lee v. Madigan*, 358 U.S. at 230; *Ludecke v. Watkins*, 335 U.S. 160, 169–170 (1948), citing *United States v. Anderson*, 9 Wall. 56, 70; *Woods v. Cloyd W. Miller Co.*, 333 U.S. 138, 141–44 (1948), quoting *Hamilton v. Kentucky Distilleries Co.*, 251 U.S. 146, 161 (1919).

In *Hamilton v. Kentucky Distilleries Co.*, 251 U.S. 146 (1919) and *Ruppert v. Caffey*, 251 U.S. 264 (1920), the Court held that liquor regulation under the War-Time Prohibition Act was constitutional after World War I hostilities had ended. Finding continuing war-related power in *Hamilton*, the Court suggested that "the power is not limited to victories in the field and the dispersion of the [insurgent] [sic] forces. It carries with it inherently the power to guard against the immediate renewal of the conflict, and to remedy the evils which have arisen from its rise and progress." 251 U.S. at 161–62, quoting *Stewart v. Kahn*, 78 U.S. 493, 507 (1870). See also "Prohibition and the War Power," *Harvard Law Review* 33, no. 6 (1920): 585–87. On prohibition, I benefitted from a paper by Heather Schafroth, Harvard Law School class of 2008.

11. *Lee v. Madigan*, 358 U.S. at 231–32, 236, citing *United States v. Anderson*, 9 Wall. 56, 69. Douglas distinguished *Woods* and *Hamilton* on the basis that "these cases deal with the reach of the war power as a source of regulatory authority over national affairs, in the aftermath of hostilities," while *Madigan* concerned courts-martial for capital offenses. 358 U.S. at 231–32. John F. O'Connor argues that the case reflected "the Court's skepticism as to the utility of the institution of courts-martial." John F. O'Connor, "The Origins and Application of the Military Deference Doctrine," *Georgia Law Review* 35 (Fall 2000): 205.

The problem of the legal end to war has reappeared in post-9/11 scholarship. Stephen I. Vladeck, "*Ludecke's* Lengthening Shadow: The Disturbing Prospect of War without End," *Journal of National Security Law and Policy* 2 (Winter 2006): 53–110; John M. Hagan, "From the XYZ Affair to the War on Terror: The Justiciability of Time of War," *Washington & Lee Law Review* 61 (Summer 2004): 1327–1383; John Alan Cohan, "Legal War: When Does It Exist, and When Does It End?" *Hastings International & Comparative Law Review* 27 (Winter 2004): 221–318. The ending of war under international law is discussed in Leslie C. Green, *The Contemporary Law of Armed Conflict*, 3rd ed. (Manchester, U.K.: Manchester University Press, 2008), 104–8.

12. Houlgate, "Drop in Crime Brings End to Army Prison at Lompoc," 30.

13. Waldo Heinrichs, *Threshold of War: Franklin D. Roosevelt and American Entry into World War II* (New York: Oxford University Press, 1988), 3; Emily Rosenberg, *A Date Which Will Live: Pearl Harbor and American Memory* (Durham, NC: Duke University Press, 2003), 15.

14. Heinrichs, *Threshold of War*, 3; Edward S. Corwin, *Total War and the Constitution* (New York: Knopf, 1947), 22, 32.

15. Corwin, *Total War and the Constitution*, 22–25; David Reynolds, *From Munich to Pearl Harbor: Roosevelt's America and the Origins of the Second World War* (Chicago: Dee, 2001), 63–68.

16. Robert H. Jackson, *That Man: An Insider's Portrait of Franklin D. Roosevelt*, John Q. Barrett, ed. (New York: Oxford University Press, 2003), 106–7; Barrett, "December 8, 1941," 75, 80–81 (quoting Phillips-Jackson interviews, 921–22).

17. Heinrichs, *Threshold of War*, 9–10; Corwin, *Total War and the Constitution*, 26–27; "President Informs the Congress of the Exchange of Certain United States Over-age Destroyers for British Naval and Air Bases; and Transmits the Correspondence and the Opinion of the Attorney-General Relative Thereto," September 3, 1940, in *The Public Papers and Addresses of Franklin D. Roosevelt 1940 Volume* (New York: Macmillan, 1941), 396; Robert H. Jackson to President Roosevelt, August 27, 1940, attached to "President Informs the Congress"; Jackson, *That Man*, 81–103. On the Neutrality Acts, see Louis Fisher, Presidential War Power, 2nd ed. (Lawrence: University Press of Kansas, 2004), 73–75.

18. Frank Murphy, *Annual Report of the Attorney General of the United States, 1939* (Washington, DC: U.S. Government Printing Office, 1939), 61–62; Robert Jackson, *Annual Report of the Attorney General of the United States, 1940* (Washington, DC: U.S. Government Printing Office, 1940), 1, 74–77; Francis Biddle, *Annual Report of the Attorney General of the United States, 1941* (Washington, DC: U.S. Government Printing Office, 1942), 6, 86–87.

19. Paul Murphy, *The Constitution in Crisis Times* (New York: Harper & Row, 1972), 216–17, quoting Jackson, *Annual Report of the Attorney General, 1940* (Washington, 1941), 1–2; Act of March 28, 1940, ch. 72, 54 Stat. 79 (1940), amending Espionage Act of 1917; Alien Registration (Smith) Act of 1940, ch. 439, 54 Stat. 670 (1940); Reynolds, *From Munich to Pearl Harbor*, 5; Douglas M. Charles, *J. Edgar Hoover and the Anti-Interventionists: FBI Political Surveillance*

and the Rise of the Domestic Security State, 1939–1945 (Columbus: Ohio State University Press, 2007), 11–12.

20. "Annual Message to the Congress," January 6, 1941, in *The Public Papers and Addresses of Franklin D. Roosevelt 1940 Volume* (New York: Macmillan, 1941), 672.

21. Alan P. Dobson, *US Wartime Aid to Britain, 1940–1946* (New York: St. Martin's, 1986); Warren F. Kimball, *The Most Unsordid Act: Lend-Lease, 1941* (Baltimore: Johns Hopkins Press, 1969); Heinrichs, *Threshold of War*, 30, 48–49.

22. "'Light of Democracy Must Be Kept Burning'—Address at Annual Dinner of White House Correspondents' Association," March 15, 1941, in *The Public Papers and Addresses of Franklin D. Roosevelt 1941 Volume* (New York: Harper & Brothers, 1950), 62, 64.

23. "'We Choose Human Freedom'—A Radio Address Announcing the Proclamation of an Unlimited National Emergency," May 27, 1941, in *The Public Papers and Addresses of Franklin D. Roosevelt 1941 Volume* (New York: Harper & Brothers, 1950), 185; Heinrichs, *Threshold of War*, 51.

24. Roosevelt, "We Choose Human Freedom."

25. Ibid.

26. "The President Proclaims That an Unlimited National Emergency Confronts the Country. Proclamation No. 2487," May 27, 1941, in *The Public Papers and Addresses of Franklin D. Roosevelt 1941 Volume* (New York: Harper & Brothers, 1950), 195; Heinrich, *Threshold of War*, 78–91.

27. Hearings before the Joint Committee on the Investigation of the Pearl Harbor Attack, Part 11, April 9, 11, May 23, 31, 1946 (Testimony of Henry Stimson), 1521–22, 5430.

28. Ibid., 5438.

29. "Stimson's Statement about Pearl Harbor and Views about the Persons Who Were to Blame," *New York Times*, March 22, 1946, 14–15; "'December 7, 1941—A Date Which Will Live in Infamy'—Address to the Congress Asking That a State of War Be Declared between the United States and Japan," December 8, 1941, in *The Public Papers and Addresses of Franklin D. Roosevelt 1941 Volume* (New York: Harper & Brothers, 1950), 514, 515; "Message to the Congress Asking

That a State of War Be Recognized between Germany and Italy and the United States," December 11, 1941, in *The Public Papers and Addresses of Franklin D. Roosevelt 1941 Volume* (New York: Harper & Brothers, 1950), 532; Corwin, *Total War and the Constitution*, 33–34.

30. Rosenberg, *A Day Which Will Live*, 14–15.
31. Hearings before the Joint Committee on the Investigation of the Pearl Harbor Attack, 5418.
32. James B. Reston, "Capital Swings into War Stride; Throngs Cheer for the President," *New York Times*, December 9, 1941, 5, quoted in Barrett, "December 8, 1941," 2; Rosenberg, *A Day Which Will Live*, 15; John W. Dower, *Cultures of War: Pearl Harbor, Hiroshima, 9/11, Iraq* (New York: Norton, 2010), 138–39.
33. "Message to the Congress Asking for Quick Action to Stabilize the Economy," September 7, 1942, in *The Public Papers and Addresses of Franklin D. Roosevelt 1942 Volume* (New York: Harper & Brothers, 1950), 364; Murphy, *The Constitution in Crisis Times*, 221–22; Jacobus TenBroek, Edward Norton Barnhart, and Floyd W. Matson, *Prejudice, War, and the Constitution* (1968), 68–184; Peter Irons, *Justice at War: The Story of the Japanese-American Internment Cases* (1983), 206–218.
34. John Q. Barrett, "December 8, 1941," 2, http://www.stjohns.edu/media/3/8ce436e990bc466dba7e7863bc178 1bb.pdf; Melvin I. Urofsky, "The Court at War and the War at the Court," *Journal of Supreme Court History*, (1996): 1–18; Melvin I. Urofsky, *Division and Discord: The Supreme Court under Stone and Vinson, (1941–1953)* (Columbia: University of South Carolina Press, 1999), 47; Murphy, *The Constitution in Crisis Times*, 238.
35. Jackson, *That Man*, 106–7; Barrett, "December 8, 1941," 4; Urofsky, "The Court at War, and the War at the Court," 1–3.
36. Murphy, *The Constitution in Crisis Times*, 213–19, 246.
37. Ibid., 172–74, quoting Kirk H. Porter and Donald B. Johnson, *National Party Platforms, 1840–1964* (Urbana: University of Illinois Press, 1966), 383; David Bixby, "The Roosevelt Court, Democratic Ideology, and Minority Rights: Another

Look at *United States v. Classic,*" *Yale Law Journal* 90 (March 1981): 747–49.

38. Reorganization of the Federal Judiciary, Hearings on S. 1392, 75th Cong., 1st Sess. (1937) (Statement of Dorothy Thompson), 860, 864; Bixby, "The Roosevelt Court, Democratic Ideology, and Minority Rights, 747–49; Jeff Shesol, *Supreme Power: Franklin Roosevelt vs. the Supreme Court* (New York: Norton, 2010), 49–50, 303; "Rome Sees Trend to Fascism In Roosevelt's Court Move," *Washington Post,* February 7, 1937, 1.

39. *De Jonge v. Oregon,* 299 U.S. 353 (1937); *Herdon v. Lowry,* 301 U.S. 242 (1937); Alfred H. Kelly, Winfred A. Harbison, and Herman Belz, *The American Constitution: Its Origins and Development,* 7th ed. (New York: Norton, 1991), 2:257–58.

40. Shawn Francis Peters, *Judging Jehovah's Witnesses: Religious Persecution and the Dawn of the Rights Revolution* (Lawrence: University Press of Kansas, 2000), 22–28, 35–38.

41. *Lovell v. Griffin,* 303 U.S. 444 (1938); *Schneider v. Irvington,* 308 U.S. 147 (1939); Murphy, *The Constitution in Crisis Times,* 195–96; *Minersville School District v. Gobitis,* 310 U.S. 586 (1940). Lillian and William's last name is misspelled in court documents. Although "Gobitis" is in the case name, the correct spelling of their name is "Gobitas." Peters, *Judging Jehovah's Witnesses,* 301–2n17.

42. *Gobitis,* 310 U.S. at 586; Peters, *Judging Jehovah's Witnesses,* 48, 52–55; 69–70; Richard Danzig, "How Questions Begot Answers in Felix Frankfurter's First Flag Salute Opinion," *Supreme Court Review* (1977): 257–74; Frankfurter to Roosevelt, Washington, D.C., May 26, 1940, in *Roosevelt and Frankfurter: Their Correspondence, 1928–1945,* ed. Max Freedman (Boston: Little, Brown, 1967), 523; Kennedy, *Freedom from Fear,* 426–27, 438–43; Friedman, *American Law in the Twentieth Century,* 282–84; Murphy, *The Constitution in Crisis Times,* 197.

43. *Gobitis,* 310 U.S. at 586, 595–96, 598; Peters, *Judging Jehovah's Witnesses,* 48, 52–55, 69–99; Danzig, "How Questions Begot Answers." The reference to Lincoln comes from Abraham Lincoln, "Special Session Message, July 4, 1861,"

in *A Compilation of the Messages and Papers of the Presidents, 1789–1897*, vol. 6, ed. James D. Richardson (Washington: Government Printing Office, 1896), 23.

44. Murphy, *The Constitution in Crisis Times*, 199–200.
45. *Jones v. Opelika*, 316 U.S. 584, 623 (1942); *West Virginia State Board of Education v. Barnette*, 319 U.S. 624, 636 (1943). The Court's first reversal in Jehovah's Witness cases came a month before *Barnette*, as the Court struck down a ban on door-to-door peddling. *Murdock v. Pennsylvania*, 319 U.S. 105 (1943).
46. Ibid., 640–41.
47. *Minersville School District v. Gobitis*, 310 U.S. 586 (1940); *West Virginia State Board of Education v. Barnette*, 319 U.S. 624, 641 (1943); Mark Graber, "Counter-Stories: Maintaining and Expanding Civil Liberties in Wartime," in *The Constitution in Wartime: Beyond Alarmism and Complacency*, ed. Mark Tushnet (Durham, NC: Duke University Press, 2005), 96. Richard A. Primus argues that the change from *Gobitis* to *Barnette* can be explained by the Court's concerns about Nazism in *Barnette*, a concern he implies was new in that case. Richard A. Primus, *The American Language of Rights* (Cambridge: Cambridge University Press, 1999), 197–99. Decided in 1940, *Gobitis* is too early to be included in the data set for Epstein et al.'s analysis of the impact of World War II on the Court, placing the case in a non-war time period against which the Court's actions during World War II are compared. Lee Epstein, Daniel E. Ho, Gary King, and Jeffrey A. Segal, "The Supreme Court during Crisis: How War Affects Only Non-War Cases," *New York University Law Review* 80 (April 2005): 46–47. Other scholars, in contrast, view *Gobitis* as affected by the context of war. Peters, *Judging Jehovah's Witnesses*, 48, 52–55, 69–70; Lawrence Friedman, *American Law in the Twentieth Century* (New Haven, CT: Yale University Press, 2002), 282–84; Murphy, *The Constitution in Crisis Times*, 197; Danzig, "How Questions Begot Answers;" Gordon Silverstein and John Hanley, "The Supreme Court and Public Opinion in Times of War and Crisis," *Hastings Law Journal* 61 (July 2010): 1453–1502.

Robert Tsai suggests that Jackson drew on President Roosevelt's idea of the "Four Freedoms," and that Roosevelt's influence was important to the outcome of the case. Robert L. Tsai, "Reconsidering *Gobitis*: An Exercise in Presidential Leadership," *Washington University Law Review* 86 (November 2008): 363–443.

48. Another example is the importance of Cold War foreign relations to civil rights reform, including *Brown v. Board of Education*. The Justice Department argued in its *amicus* brief in *Brown* that "the existence of discrimination against minority groups in the United States has an adverse effect upon our relations with other countries." Brief for the United States as *Amicus Curiae, Brown v. Board of Education* (1954), p. 6 (filed in 1952). Thousands of State Department documents from the era detail the way race discrimination harmed the U.S. image around the world, undermining the American Cold War mission. Mary L. Dudziak, *Cold War Civil Rights: Race and the Image of American Democracy* (Princeton, NJ: Princeton University Press, 2000); Mary L. Dudziak, "*Brown* as a Cold War Case," *Journal of American History* 91 (June 2004): 32–42; Thomas Borstelmann, *The Cold War and the Color Line: American Race Relations in the Global Arena* (Cambridge, MA: Harvard University Press, 2001). Scholarship on civil rights and foreign relations has been pulled back into the time zone analysis. It is more accurate to see this work as a challenge to the idea that war/security-related impacts are limited to time zones rather than as a reinforcement of it.

49. John W. Dower, *Embracing Defeat: Japan in the Wake of World War II* (New York: Norton, 1999), 39–44.

50. Tom Brokaw, *The Greatest Generation*, 2nd ed. (New York: Random House, 2004), xxvii; Stephen Ambrose, *Band of Brothers: E Company, 506th Regiment, 101st Airborne from Normandy to Hitler's Eagle's Nest* (New York: Simon & Schuster, 2001); Mikael Salomon (director), *Band of Brothers* (HBO miniseries, 2010). For a critical appraisal of the way World War II is remembered, see Marianna Torgovnick, *The*

War Complex: World War II in Our Time (Chicago: University of Chicago Press, 2005).

51. Jeffrey Record, "The American Way of War: Cultural Barriers to Successful Counterinsurgency," The Cato Institute, Policy Analysis no. 577, September 1, 2006, http://www.cato.org/pub_display.php?pub_id=6640; Brent C. Bankus, "We've Done This Before," *Small Wars Journal* 4 (February 2006): 33–36. See also M. W. Shervington, "A Hundred Years of Irregular Warfare," *Small Wars Journal* 4 (February 2006): 1–45. For an example of traditional ideas about wartime in legal scholarship, see Bruce Ackerman, "This Is Not a War," *Yale Law Journal* 113 (June 2004): 1871–1907, 1872.

Chapter 3

1. James M. Markham, "American Officer Killed by Russian in East Germany," *New York Times*, March 26, 1985, A–1; John J. Miller, "Our Last Cold War Casualty," *National Review*, April 5, 2004, 39–40.
2. Miller, "Our Last Cold War Casualty," 40.
3. Ibid.
4. Markham, "American Officer Killed"; Reuters, "'Caught Spying': Soviet Guard Kills U.S. Army Officer," *The Globe & Mail*, March 25, 1985; "Soviets Say Major Was Spy: But Weinberger Calls Death of U.S. Officer 'Unjustified,'" *San Diego Union-Tribune*, March 27, 1985, A–1; "Major Slain Taking Photos through Window: Soviets: Sentry Acted Properly, They Insist," *Los Angeles Times*, March 26, 1985, 1; "U.S. Says Shooting Was Not Justified," *New York Times*, March 26, 1985, A–4; Lou Cannon and David Hoffman "Gorbachev Responds to Summit Bid: Reagan's Aides Describe Written Reply as Positive," *Los Angeles Times*, April 2, 1985, 1.
5. Bernard Gwertzman., "U.S. Plans to Seek Closer Soviet Ties In Spite of Slaying," *New York Times*, March 27, 1985, A–1; Miller, "Our Last Cold War Casualty," 41; Robert C. Toth, "Geneva Talks Focus on Space: U.S., Soviets Concentrate on This Weapons Issue," *Los Angeles Times*, March 27, 1985, 22.

6. "Body of Slain Major Flown Back Home," *Houston Chronicle*, March 30, 1985, 8; Don Shannon and Doyle McManus, "Slain Major's Body Brought Home," *Los Angeles Times*, March 30, 1985, 2.

7. Site of the Shooting of Major Arthur D. Nicholson Jr., U.S. Military Liaison Mission webpage, http://www.usmlm.org/home/nicholson/ludwigslust.htm.

8. Arthur D. Nicholson Jr., Arlington National Cemetery website, http://www.arlingtoncemetery.net/nicholsn.htm; Richard Fournier, "Cold War Casualties Cry Out for Commemoration," *VFW Magazine* 91 (May 2004), 28.

9. Carl von Clausewitz, *On War*, trans. Michael Howard and Peter Paret (Princeton, NJ: Princeton University Press, 1984).

10. Mike Moore, "Midnight Never Come," *Bulletin of Atomic Scientists* 51 (November 1995): 16–27; Bob Hanke, "Speed," *Semiotic Review of Books* 15, no. 2 (2005): 1–12; Doomsday Clock Timeline, *Bulletin of the Atomic Scientists*, http://www.thebulletin.org/content/doomsday-clock/timeline.

   John-Francis Phipps argues that "The bomb is a time bomb: it personifies time in the sense of providing the capacity for creating the biggest ever bang in time, a nuclear apocalypse in an otherwise empty space, a cataclysmic man-made event." John-Francis Phipps, *Time and the Bomb* (Oxford: Pica Press, 1982), 8.

11. George Orwell, "You and the Atomic Bomb," Nuclear Age Peace Foundation, http://www.wagingpeace.org/articles/0000/1945_orwell_you-and-the-bomb.htm (originally published October 19, 1945).

12. Bernard Baruch, "Text of Bernard Baruch's Address at Portrait Unveiling," *New York Times*, April 17, 1947, 21; Walter Lippmann, "Today and Tomorrow, The Cold War: Study of U.S. Policy," *Washington Post*, September 2, 1947, 11; Walter Lippmann, *The Cold War: A Study in U.S. Foreign Policy* (New York: Harper, 1947). For post-9/11 references to the Cold War era, see, e.g., David Cole, "The New McCarthyism: Repeating History in the War on Terrorism," *Harvard Civil Rights-Civil Liberties Law Review* 38 (Winter 2003): 1–30;

Elaine Tyler May, "Echoes of the Cold War: The Aftermath of September 11," in *September 11 in History: A Watershed Moment?* ed. Mary L. Dudziak (Durham, NC: Duke University Press, 2003), 38–40.

13. Jeffrey Record, "The American Way of War: Cultural Barriers to Successful Counterinsurgency," The Cato Institute, Policy Analysis no. 577, September 1, 2006, http://www.cato.org/pub_display.php?pub_id=6640. For an example of a traditional conception of wartime in legal scholarship, see Bruce Ackerman, "This Is Not a War," *Yale Law Journal* 113 (June 2004): 1871–1907; Geoffrey Stone, *Perilous Times: Free Speech in Wartime from the Sedition Act of 1879 to the War on Terrorism* (New York: Norton, 2005); William Rehnquist, *All the Laws but One: Civil Liberties in Wartime* (New York: Knopf, 1998). For a contrary view, see Mark Brandon, "War and the American Constitutional Order," *Vanderbilt Law Review* 56 (November 2003): 1815–65.

Critics of American military planning argue that weapons systems and military training are based on a traditional conception of wartime, which is at odds with the actual contemporary American warfare. Record, "The American Way of War"; Brent C. Bankus, "We've Done This Before," *Small Wars Journal* 4 (February 2006): 33–36. See also M. W. Shervington, "A Hundred Years of Irregular Warfare," *Small Wars Journal* 4 (February 2006): 1–45.

14. Stone, *Perilous Times*, 311; Cass Sunstein, "Judicial Minimalism in War," *Supreme Court Review* (2004): 47–109, 48; Kim Lane Scheppele, "Law in a Time of Emergency: States of Exception and the Temptations of 9/11," *University of Pennsylvania Journal of Constitutional Law* 6 (May 2004): 1001–83.

15. Dwight Macdonald, "The 'Decline to Barbarism'" (1945), in Barton Bernstein, ed., *The Atomic Bomb: The Critical Issues* (New York: Little Brown, 1976). See Paul Boyer, *The Bomb's Early Light: American Thought and Culture at the Dawn of the Atomic Age*, 2nd ed. (Chapel Hill: University of North Carolina Press, 1994).

16. *On the Beach* (1959), directed by Stanley Kramer.

17. Michael J. Hogan, *A Cross of Iron: Harry S. Truman and the Origins of the National Security State, 1945–1954* (New York: Cambridge University Press, 1998), 24.

18. Ibid., 209, 215–17, 234, 265, 300, 313. See also Campbell Craig and Fredrik Logevall, *America's Cold War: The Politics of Insecurity* (Cambridge, MA: Harvard University Press, 2009).

19. National Security Act of 1947, P.L. 80–235, 61 Stat 496 (1947); Hogan, *Cross of Iron*; Steven Casey, *Selling the Korean War: Propaganda, Politics, and Public Opinion in the United States, 1950–1953* (New York: Oxford University Press, 2007); Marilyn Young, "Ground Zero: Enduring War," in *September 11 in History: A Watershed Moment?* ed. Mary L. Dudziak (Durham, NC: Duke University Press, 2003). There are many works on the Korean War. William Stueck emphasizes the multilateral nature of the war in William Stueck, *The Korean War: An International History* (Princeton, NJ: Princeton University Press, 1997).

20. Colin S. Gray, "The American Way of War: Critique and Implications," in *Rethinking the Principles of War*, ed. Anthony D. McIvor (Annapolis, MD: Naval Institute Press, 2005), quoted in Record, "The American Way of War," 3–4. A consequence of this, for Gray, is that "the U.S. military has a long history of waging war for the goal of victory, paying scant regard to the consequences of the course of its operations for the character of the peace that will follow." Ibid.

Brent C. Bankus finds a similar tendency in military training. "While the US military (past and present) spends most of its time involved in Military Operations Other Than War (MOOTW), or Small Scale Contingencies, the training focus is traditional symmetric operations—for example a major theater of war." Bankus, "We've Done This Before," 33. Similarly, Jeffrey Record has written that "since the early 1940s, the Army has trained, equipped, and organized for large-scale conventional operations against like adversaries, and it has traditionally employed conventional military operations even against irregular enemies." Record, "The American Way of War," 1.

21. Kenneth Osgood, *Total Cold War: Eisenhower's Secret Propaganda Battle at Home and Abroad* (Lawrence: University Press of Kansas, 2006), 1–2.

22. Odd Arne Westad, *The Global Cold War: Third World Interventions and the Making of Our Times* (Cambridge: Cambridge University Press, 2005), 2; Odd Arne Westad, "Introduction: Reviewing the Cold War," in *Reviewing the Cold War: Approaches, Interpretations, Theory*, ed. Odd Arne Westad (London: Frank Cass, 2000), 1; Lori Lynn Bogle, "Introduction," in *The Cold War, Volume 1: Origins of the Cold War*, ed. Lori Lynn Bogle (New York: Routledge, 2001), vii; Lori Lynn Bogle, "Introduction," in *The Cold War, Volume 3: Hot Wars of the Cold War*, ed. Lori Lynn Bogle (New York: Routledge, 2001), vii; Robert J. McMahon, *The Cold War on the Periphery: The United States, India, and Pakistan* (New York: Columbia University Press, 1994); Anders Stephanson, "Fourteen Notes on the Very Concept of the Cold War," *H-Diplo*, http://www.h-net.org/~diplo/essays/PDF/stephanson-14notes.pdf. According to Westad, the Soviets "never used the term officially before the Gorbachev era, since they clung to the fiction that their country was 'peaceful' and only 'imperialism' was aggressive." Westad, *Global Cold War*, 2.

23. David Anderson, *Red Continent: The Cold War in Africa* (London: Faber & Faber, forthcoming); Christopher Bayley and Tim Harper, *Forgotten Wars: Freedom and Revolution in Southeast Asia* (London: Penguin, 2006), xxvii; Eric Hobsbawm, *The Age of Extremes: A History of the World, 1914–1991* (New York: Pantheon, 1995), 5.

Stephen F. Cohen, historian of the Soviet Union, challenges the traditional periodization, finding origins in the initial framework of U.S.-Soviet relations after 1917, and arguing that Cold War dynamics persist in continuing U.S.-Russian relations. As a result, for Cohen, 1989 was not an ending, but instead a new chapter in what we call the Cold War. Stephen F. Cohen, *Soviet Fates and Lost Alternatives: From Stalinism to the New Cold War* (New York: Columbia University Press, 2009).

24. National Defense Authorization Act for Fiscal Year 1998, S. 936, 105th Cong. Sec. 535 (1997); "The Cold War Victory Medal—Long Overdue!" American Cold War Veterans, http://www.americancoldwarvets.org/victory_medal.html; Armed Forces Expeditionary Medal, Institute of Heraldry, Office of the Administrative Assistant to the Secretary of the Army, http://www.tioh.hqda.pentagon.mil/Awards/af_expeditionary.aspx.
    The time period covered by the Cold War Medal has sometimes differed. The first bill defined the Cold War as the period from August 15, 1974, through December 21, 1991, and another from August 14, 1945, through November 9, 1989. Most proposals, however, have specified the time period as September 2, 1945, through December 26, 1991. S. Amend. 743 to National Defense Authorization Act for Fiscal Year 1998, S. 936, 105th Cong. § 535 (1997); An act to authorize appropriations for fiscal year 2000 for military activities of the Department of Defense, to prescribe personnel strengths for such fiscal year for the Armed Forces, and for other purposes, S. 1060, 106th Cong. § 1086 (1999) (unenacted); S. Amdt. 474 and S. 534 to National Defense Authorization Act for Fiscal Year 2000, S. 1059, 106th Cong. § 1086 (1999) (unenacted); Commemoration of the Victory of Freedom in the Cold War Act, H.R. 2440, 106th Cong. §§ 1, 2 (1999) (unenacted).

25. S. Amend. 2163 National Defense Authorization Act for Fiscal Year 2008, H.R. 1585, 110th Cong. § 556 (2007) (unenacted); "Cold War Certificate Approved," Department of Defense News Release, April 5, 1999, http://www.defense.gov/releases/release.aspx?releaseid=2031.

26. "VFW Eligibility Information," October 2005, Veterans of Foreign Wars, http://www.vfw.org/resources/pdf/eligibility05.pdf. For the Veterans of Foreign Wars, the Cold War years count for membership not on the basis of the Cold War itself, but of more precise military engagements from World War II until the 1990s.

27. Manning Marable, *Race, Reform, and Rebellion: The Second Reconstruction in Black America, 1945–2006* (Jackson, MS:

University Press of Mississippi, 2007), 13; Alan Brinkley, "World War II and American Liberalism," in *The War in American Culture: Society and Consciousness during World War II*, ed. Lewis A. Erenberg and Susan E. Hirsch (Chicago: University of Chicago Press, 1996), 313–330; Robert Cowley, "Introduction," in *The Cold War: A Military History*, ed. Robert Cowley (New York: Random House, 2006), xvi.

Marable writes powerfully about the impact of war on the writing of history itself. In spite of the impact of the war of World War II, he writes, "people who thought as I did were called upon in 1945 to treat the postwar era with intellectual and critical tools more applicable to the vanished world of the thirties—a world we had never had time to understand as we lived it." Marable, *Race, Reform, and Rebellion*, 13.

28. Ellen Schrecker, *Many Are the Crimes: McCarthyism in America* (Boston: Little, Brown, 1998); Michal R. Belknap, *Cold War Political Justice: The Smith Act and the Communist Party* (Westport, CT: Greenwood, 1977); Gerald Horne, *Black and Red: W.E.B. Du Bois and the Afro-American Response to the Cold War* (Albany: State University of New York Press, 1985). For Schrecker, the reason that the domestic repression happened in the United States and not other nations affected by the Cold War stemmed not from geopolitics, but from developments in Washington, DC, where "anticommunist activists like J. Edgar Hoover seized the opportunity presented by the deepening antagonism to the Soviet Union to sell their supposed expertise about Communism to the rest of the political establishment." Schrecker, *Many Are the Crimes*, xiv–xv.

29. Lynn Hunt, *Measuring Time, Making History* (Budapest: Central European University Press, 2008), 70–71.

30. Michal Belknap, *Cold War Political Justice: The Smith Act, the Communist Party, and American Civil Liberties* (Westport, CT: Greenwood Press, 1977), 5–7; Scott Martelle, *The Fear Within: Spies, Commies, and American Democracy on Trial* (New Brunswick, NJ: Rutgers University Press, 2011); *Dennis v. United States*, 341 U.S. 494 (1950).

31. Belknap, *Cold War Political Justice*, 5–7; *Dennis v. United States*, 341 U.S. 494, 588–589 (1950), Douglas, J., dissenting.
32. *Yates v. United States*, 354 U.S. 298 (1957); *Aptheker v. Secretary of State*, 378 U.S. 500 (1964); Lucas A. Powe, *The Warren Court and American Politics* (Cambridge, MA: Harvard University Press, 2002); Belknap, *Cold War Political Justice*, 5–7; Stone, *Perilous Times*, 252–54; Schrecker, *Many Are the Crimes*, xvi. In 1961 a divided Court upheld a finding of the Subversive Activities Control Board that the Communist Party of the United States was a "Communist action organization" dominated and directed by the Soviet Union, and so required to register with the board as a subversive organization. *Communist Party of the United States v. Subversive Activities Control Bd. No. 12*, 367 U.S. 1 (1961), and in another 5–4 split, the Court also upheld the prosecution of Julius Scales for being an active member of the Communist Party, in violation of the Smith Act, but unanimously overturned John Francis Noto's Smith Act conviction, finding insufficient evidence of active advocacy of overthrow of the government. *Scales v. United States*, 367 U.S. 203 (1961); *Noto v. United States*, 367 U.S. 290 (1961).

Focusing specifically on political repression, Robert Justin Goldstein shows repression deepening and waning during different moments in the Cold War. He argues that increases in repression are tied principally to "hot wars," so that there is less repression from the end of the Korean War until Vietnam. But for his model to work, the Cold War becomes the functional equivalent of a hot war, since he sees the era from 1946 to 1954 as producing increased repression. And he limits the Vietnam era to 1965 to 1975, even though the United States was deeply engaged in Vietnam before the Gulf of Tonkin incident. Robert Justin Goldstein, *Political Repression in Modern America: From 1870 to 1976* (Urbana-Champaign: University of Illinois Press, 2001). On Vietnam, see Marilyn B. Young, *The Vietnam Wars, 1945–1990* (New York: HarperCollins, 1991); Robert J. McMahon, *The Limits of Empire: The United States and Southeast Asia since World War II* (New York: Columbia University Press, 1999).

33. Thomas I. Emerson, *A System of Freedom of Expression* (New York: Random House, 1970), 55–56; Eric J. Leed, *No Man's Land: Conflict and Identity in World War I* (Cambridge: Cambridge University Press, 1979), 129.

34. Stone, *Perilous Times*, 311. Stone's quote is from William M. Wiecek, "The Legal Foundations of Domestic Anticommunism: The Background of *Dennis v. United States*," *Supreme Court Review* (2001): 375, 417. The end point in 1957 for Stone is the Supreme Court ruling in *Yates*.

    Cass Sunstein also treats the Cold War as if it was a war in "Judicial Minimalism in War," however he gives it a different time span. For Sunstein, judicial minimalism is when judges do "no more than necessary to resolve cases." To explore the role of minimalism in cases involving trade-offs between rights and national security, he takes up Supreme Court cases decided during the Civil War, World War I, World War II, the Cold War, and the war on terrorism. One of his examples is *Kent v. Dulles*, a 1958 case involving denial of a passport to Rockwell Kent, who hoped to travel to England and Helsinki, Finland, to attend a meeting of the World Council of Peace. Kent's passport was denied because he was allegedly a member of the Communist Party. The passport office asked Kent to submit an affidavit regarding his Communist Party affiliation, and he refused, arguing that the affidavit requirement was illegal. Although an expansive opinion would have been possible, Sunstein notes that the Court instead adopted narrow grounds, holding that the passport denial "was beyond the statutory authority of the Secretary of State." "Proceeding in minimalist fashion," Sunstein argues, "the Court left undecided the question whether Congress could constitutionally give that authority to the President. The advantage of the minimalist approach is that it reflects commendable uncertainty about difficult questions, enlisting political safeguards as the first line of defense against unjustified intrusions on freedom." Although Sunstein's focus is wartime, he variously discusses "times of war" and times when the nation's security is threatened. Sunstein, "Judicial Minimalism in War," 48.

In an analysis of the impact of crisis on judicial decision-making, Harry Edwards compares the Cold War to World War II, but doesn't explicitly argue that the Cold War was a "war." "Like World War II," he writes, "the Cold War claimed serious constitutional casualties on the domestic front. In a climate made almost hysterical by fear of communist infiltration, the Government engaged in battle against ideas, waging war against speech and associational activities seen as dangerously disloyal. . . . The Court's Cold War experience with seditious speech, for instance, interrupted the development of free speech doctrine so thoroughly that recovery took close to twenty years." Harry T. Edwards, "The Judicial Function and the Elusive Goal of Principled Decisionmaking," *Wisconsin Law Review* 1 (1991): 837–65, 844–45.

35. Michael Dobbs, *One Minute to Midnight: Kennedy, Khrushchev, and Castro on the Brink of Nuclear War* (New York: Knopf, 2008); *Engle v. Vitale*, 370 U.S. 421 (1962); *Baker v. Carr*, 369 U.S. 186 (1962); Powe, *The Warren Court*.

36. Eric A. Posner and Adrian Vermeule, *Terror in the Balance: Security, Liberty, and the Courts* (New York: Oxford University Press, 2007), 42.

37. Emerson, *A System of Freedom of Expression*, 56; Stephen M. Feldman, *Free Expression and Democracy: A History* (Chicago: The University of Chicago Press, 2008), 432–33. See also Stephen J. Whitfield, *The Culture of the Cold War*, 2nd ed. (Baltimore: Johns Hopkins University Press, 1996), 4–5.

38. Adam J. Berinsky, *In Time of War: Understanding American Public Opinion from World War II to Iraq* (Chicago: The University of Chicago Press, 2009). There is new work on law and public opinion, however it does engage this recent political science literature. See Barry Friedman, *The Will of the People: How Public Opinion has Influenced the Supreme Court* (New York: Farrar, Straus and Giroux, 2009).

39. Julian E. Zelizer, *Arsenal of Democracy: The Politics of National Security—From World War II to the War on Terrorism* (New York: Basic Books, 2010), 506–7.

40. E.g., Mary L. Dudziak, *Cold War Civil Rights: Race and the Image of American Democracy* (Princeton, NJ: Princeton

University Press, 2000); Thomas Borstelmann, *The Cold War and the Color Line: American Race Relations in the Global Arena* (Cambridge, MA: Harvard University Press, 2001); Brenda Gayle Plummer, *Rising Wind: Black Americans and U.S. Foreign Affairs, 1935–1960* (Chapel Hill: University of North Carolina Press, 1996); Carol Anderson, *Eyes off the Prize: The United Nations and the African American Struggle for Human Rights, 1944–1955* (New York: Cambridge University Press, 2003); Penny M. Von Eschen, *Race against Empire: Black Americans and Anticolonialism, 1937–1957* (Ithaca, NY: Cornell University Press, 1997); Jonathan Rosenberg, *How Far the Promised Land?: World Affairs and the American Civil Rights Movement from the First World War to Vietnam* (Princeton, NJ: Princeton University Press, 2005); Michael L. Krenn, ed., *The Impact of Race on U.S. Foreign Policy: A Reader* (New York: Garland, 1999).

The Cold War's impact on civil rights did not last through the entirety of the Cold War era. By the mid-1960s, U.S. Information Agency analysis suggested that American race relations no longer had such a negative impact on U.S. international prestige. Following the passage of important civil rights legislation, the message was finally getting through that the U.S. government was behind civil rights. Although peoples of other nations continued to believe that more had to be accomplished, American democracy now seemed less complicit in racial oppression. Ultimately the U.S. government believed that its propaganda battle had succeeded, and peoples of other nations were more likely to believe that the U.S. government supported civil rights. At the same time, other matters, especially Vietnam, drowned out the impact of civil rights on the U.S. image abroad. Dudziak, *Cold War Civil Rights*, 203–248. Cold War foreign affairs did not generate a perceived need for expanded equality rights across the board. For example, while U.S. propaganda on race emphasized equality, U.S. propaganda on women emphasized domesticity. Laura A. Belmonte, *Selling the American Way: U.S. Propaganda and the Cold War* (Philadelphia: University of Pennsylvania Press, 2008).

41. Mark Graber, "Counter-Stories: Maintaining and Expanding Civil Liberties in Wartime," in *The Constitution in Wartime: Beyond Alarmism and Complacency*, ed. Mark V. Tushnet (Durham, NC: Duke University Press, 2005).

42. Adrian R. Lewis, *The American Culture of War: The History of U.S. Military Force from World War II to Operation Iraqi Freedom* (New York: Oxford University Press, 2007), 203; Steven Casey, *Selling the Korean War: Propaganda, Politics, and Public Opinion in the United States, 1950–1953* (New York: Oxford University Press, 2007), 4–5. Paul Murphy considers the Cold War and Korea together. Murphy, *The Constitution in Crisis Times*, 279–309.

43. Stueck, *The Korean War*; Lewis, *American Culture of War*, 85–90; Casey, *Selling the Korean War*.

44. Susan A. Brewer, *Why America Fights: Patriotism and War Propaganda from the Philippines to Iraq* (New York: Oxford University Press, 2009), 142–45. See also Berinsky, *In Time of War*.

45. Young, "Ground Zero: Enduring War"; Casey, *Selling the Korean War*; Stueck, *The Korean War*.

46. *Youngstown Sheet and Tube Co. v. Sawyer*, 343 U.S. 579 (1952); Maeve Marcus, *Truman and the Steel Seizure Case: The Limits of Presidential Power* (Durham, NC: Duke University Press, 1994).

47. *Youngstown Sheet and Tube Co. v. Sawyer*, 343 U.S. 579 (1952); Neal Devins and Louis Fisher, "The Steel Seizure Case: One of a Kind?" *Constitutional Commentary* 19 (Spring 2002): 63–86.

48. Craig and Logevall, *America's Cold War*, 127; Andrew Bacevich, *The Limits of Power: The End of American Exceptionalism* (New York: Macmillan, 2009), 107; NSC 68: United States Objectives and Programs for National Security, April 7, 1950.

49. Craig and Logevall, *America's Cold War*, 127, 132–34. See also Andrew Bacevich, *Washington Rules: America's Path to Permanent War* (New York: Metropolitan Books, 2010).

50. Craig and Logevall, *America's Cold War*, 134–137. See also Hogan, *Cross of Iron*; Julian Zelizer, *Arsenal of Democracy:*

The Politics of National Security—From World War II to the War on Terrorism (New York: Basic Books, 2010).

51. See, e.g., Alfred H. Kelly, Winfred A. Harbison, and Herman Belz, *The American Constitution: Its Origins and Development*, 7th ed. (New York: Norton, 1991), 2:553–580.

52. James Ledbetter, *Unwarranted Influence: Dwight D. Eisenhower and the Military-Industrial Complex* (New Haven, CT: Yale University Press, 2011), 215–16; Craig and Logevall, *America's Cold War*, 362.

53. Marilyn Young, "Limited War, Unltd." (unpublished paper), 4. See also Catherine Lutz, *Homefront: A Military City and the American Twentieth Century* (Boston: Beacon Press, 2001).

54. Louis Fisher's pivotal work on presidential power and war takes up a more complete history of American warfare than do most scholars of law and war, but his treatment of the Cold War era focuses on *Youngstown*. Louis Fisher, *Presidential War Power*, 2nd ed. (Lawrence: University Press of Kansas, 2004). Kim Scheppele discusses the national security state in Scheppele, "Law in a Time of Emergency."

55. In her influential work, Kim Scheppele views the Cold War as a wartime, but along with Hogan, focuses on a shift in the state in the Cold War era. For Scheppele, the United States transitions to a politics of emergency, dangerously enhancing executive power. She compares the United States during the Cold War to wartime Germany. Scheppele's time frame for the Cold War mirrors the consensus periodization in diplomatic history: from after World War II to the fall of the Soviet Union in 1991. Scheppele, "Law in a Time of Emergency." Jill Elaine Hasday uses a similar periodization in "Civil War as Paradigm: Reestablishing the Rule of Law at the End of the Cold War," *Kansas Journal of Law and Public Policy*, 5 (Winter 1996) 129–52.

Chapter 4

1. David Scott, lc_story101.xml, December 17, 2003, Library of Congress Stories Series, September 11 Digital

Archive, http://911digitalarchive.org/parser.php?object_id=128; Michael Kochevar, lc_story108.xml, December 17, 2003, Library of Congress Stories Series, September 11 Digital Archive, http://911digitalarchive.org/parser.php?object_id=337; Barton W. Whitman, lc_story121.xml, December 18, 2003, Library of Congress Stories Series, September 11 Digital Archive, http://911digitalarchive.org/parser.php?object_id=311; Serdar Dalkir, lc_story124.xml, Decem ber 18, 2003, Library of Congress Stories Series, September 11 Digital Archive, http://911digitalarchive.org/parser.php?object_id=156; Jeanene Dunn, lc_story125.xml, December 18, 2003, Library of Congress Stories Series, September 11 Digital Archive, http://911digitalarchive.org/parser.php?object_id=255; Tom Neville, lc_story127.xml, December 18, 2003, Library of Congress Stories Series, September 11 Digital Archive, http://911digitalarchive.org/parser.php?object_id=95;Robert Warne, lc_story128.xml, December 18, 2003, Library of Congress Stories Series, September 11 Digital Archive, http://911digitala rchive.org/parser.php?object_id=369; Kenneth Pins, lc_story13.xml, December 18, 2003, Library of Congress Stories Series, September 11 Digital Archive, http://911digitalarchive.org/parser.php?object_id=390; Deb Young, lc_story146.xml, December 19, 2003, Library of Congress Stories Series, September 11 Digital Archive, http://911digitalarchive.org/parser.php?object_id=397; Suhad Bergman, lc_story158.xml, December 22, 2003, Library of Congress Stories Series, 11 Digital Archive, http://911digitalarchive.org/parser.php?object_id=238; John Jackson, lc_story168.xml, December 22, 2003, Library of Congress Stories Series, September 11 Digital Archive, http://911digitalarchive.org/parser.php?object_id=147; Mark Heffron, lc_story170.xml, December 24, 2003, Library of Congress Stories Series, September 11 Digital Archive, http://911digitalarchive.org/parser.php?object_id=325; Megan Jones, lc_story177.xml, December 30, 2003, Library of Congress Stories Series,

September 11 Digital Archive, http://911digitalarchive. org/parser.php?object_id=229; Meg Little, lc_story19. xml, March 5, 2003, Library of Congress Stories Series, September 11 Digital Archive, http://911digitalarchive. org/parser.php?object_id=358; Mark Smith, lc_story219. xml, January 7, 2004, Library of Congress Stories Series, September 11 Digital Archive, http://911digitalarchive. org/parser.php?object_id=388; Jodi Fayard, lc_story244. xml, January 12, 2004, Library of Congress Stories Series, September 11 Digital Archive, http://911digitalarchive. org/parser.php?object_id=181; Derrick C. Blohm, lc_ story246.xml, January 13, 2004, Library of Congress Stories Series, September 11 Digital Archive, http://911d igitalarchive.org/parser.php?object_id=184; Glenn P. Larcom, lc_story259.xml, January 15, 2004, Library of Congress Stories Series, September 11 Digital Archive, http://911digitalarchive.org/parser.php?object_id=107; William Thomas "Tom" Bowen, lc_story262.xml, January 16, 2004, Library of Congress Stories Series, September 11 Digital Archive, http://911digitalarchive.org/parser. php?object_id=309; Laura Hedien, lc_story266.xml, January 19, 2004, Library of Congress Stories Series, September 11 Digital Archive, http://911digitalarchive.org/ parser.php?object_id=197.

2. Colin Riebel, lc_story149.xml, December 20, 2003, Library of Congress Stories Series, September 11 Digital Archive, http://911digitalarchive.org/parser.php?object_ id=351; Bethany (last name withheld), lc_story255.xml, January 15, 2004, Library of Congress Stories Series, September 11 Digital Archive, http://911digitalarchive. org/parser.php?object_id=332; Kiley Clemens, lc_ story72.xml, December 14, 2003, Library of Congress Stories Series, September 11 Digital Archive, http://911digitalarchive.org/parser.php?object_id=330; Becky Funke, lc_story76.xml, December 16, 2003, Library of Congress Stories Series, September 11 Digital Archive, http://911digitalarchive.org/parser. php?object_id=131.

3. John L. Cheek Jr., lc_story102.xml, December 17, 2003, Library of Congress Stories Series, September 11 Digital Archive, http://911digitalarchive.org/parser.php?object_id=101; Ted L. Glines, lc_story120.xml, December 18, 2003, Library of Congress Stories Series, September 11 Digital Archive, http://911digitalarchive.org/parser.php?object_id=224.

4. Deb Young, lc_story146.xml, December 19, 2003, Library of Congress Stories Series, September 11 Digital Archive, http://911digitalarchive.org/parser.php?object_id=397; Herbert Ouida, lc_story74.xml, December 16, 2003, Library of Congress Stories Series, September 11 Digital Archive, http://911digitalarchive.org/parser.php?object_id=186; Debra Baron, lc_story80.xml, December 16, 2003, Library of Congress Stories Series, September 11 Digital Archive, http://911digitalarchive.org/parser.php?object_id=326; Kenneth Summers, lc_story85.xml, December 16, 2003, Library of Congress Stories Series, September 11 Digital Archive, http://911digitalarchive.org/parser.php?object_id=393 .

5. Felice Chaifetz, lc_story184.xml, January 2, 2004, Library of Congress Stories Series, September 11 Digital Archive, http://911digitalarchive.org/parser.php?object_id=148.

6. Debra Baron, lc_story80.xml, September 11 Digital Archive.

7. Diane Fairben, December 17, 2003, Library of Congress Stories Series, September 11 Digital Archive, http://911digitalarchive.org/parser.php?object_id=122; Tim McClelland, lc_story145.xml, December 19, 2003, Library of Congress Stories Series, September 11 Digital Archive, http://911digitalarchive.org/parser.php?object_id=152; Michael Burke, lc_story182.xml, December 30, 2003, Library of Congress Stories Series, September 11 Digital Archive, http://911digitalarchive.org/parser.php?object_id=336; Patricia Latessa, lc_story191.xml, January 4, 2004, Library of Congress Stories Series, September 11 Digital Archive, http://911digitalarchive.org/parser.php?object_id=304; Debra Baron, lc_story80.xml, September 11 Digital Archive.

8. Brian E. Gard, lc_story213.xml, January 6, 2004, Library of Congress Stories Series, September 11 Digital Archive, http://911digitalarchive.org/parser.php?object_id=242.

9. The City of Oklahoma City, *Alfred P. Murrah Federal Building Bombing, April 19, 1995 Final Report* (Stillwater: Fire Protection Publications, Oklahoma State University, 1996), ix; Simon Reeve, *The New Jackals: Ramzi Yousef, Osama bin Laden and the Future of Terrorism* (Boston: Northeastern University Press, 1999), 15, 105–6, 235–54; Mark S. Hamm, *Terrorism as Crime: From Oklahoma City to Al-Qaeda and Beyond* (New York: New York University Press, 2007), 49–50; Stuart A. Wright, *Patriots, Politics, and the Oklahoma City Bombing* (New York: Cambridge University Press, 2007), 195–99; Edward T. Linenthal, *The Unfinished Bombing: Oklahoma City in American Memory* (New York: Oxford University Press, 2001), 239. On the way terrorism and crime were considered separate categories, see Laurence R. Helfer, "Transforming International Law after the September 11 Attacks? Three Evolving Paradigms for Regulating International Terrorism," in *September 11 in History: A Watershed Moment?* ed. Mary L. Dudziak (Durham, NC: Duke University Press, 2003), 180–93.

10. Mary L. Dudziak, "Introduction," in *September 11 in History: A Watershed Moment?* ed. Mary L. Dudziak (Durham, NC: Duke University Press, 2003).

11. "Remarks Following a Meeting With the National Security Team," September 12, 2001, in *The Public Papers of the President of the United States: George W. Bush—2001, Book II* (Washington, DC: United States Government Printing Office, 2003), 1100; "Remarks in a Telephone Conversation with New York City Mayor Rudolph W. Giuliani and New York Governor George E. Pataki and an Exchange with Reporters," September 12, 2001, in *The Public Papers of the President of the United States: George W. Bush—2001, Book II* (Washington, DC: United States Government Printing Office, 2003), 1104. See also David Luban, "The War on Terrorism and the End of Human Rights," in *The Constitution in Wartime: Beyond Alarmism and Complacency*, ed. Mark Tushnet (Durham, NC: Duke University Press: 2005), 219–31.

12. On the history of U.S. war-related public information programs directed at the American people, see Susan Brewer,

Why America Fights: Patriotism and War Propaganda from the Philippines to Iraq (New York: Oxford University Press, 2009).

13. "Address Before a Joint Session of the Congress on the United States Response to the Terrorist Attacks of September 11," September 20, 2001, in *The Public Papers of the President of the United States: George W. Bush—2001, Book II* (Washington, DC: United States Government Printing Office, 2003), 1140–41; "Remarks at the Annual Convention of the National Association of Evangelicals in Orlando, Florida," March 8, 1983, in *The Public Papers of the President of the United States: Ronald Reagan—1983, Book I* (Washington, DC: United States Government Printing Office), 364.

14. Riad Z. Abdelkarim, "Time to Answer: Why Do They Hate Us?" September 17, 2002, *CounterPunch*, http://www.counterpunch.org/abdelkarim0917.html; Bush, "Address to a Joint Session of Congress and the American People."

15. "Address Before a Joint Session of the Congress on the United States Response to the Terrorist Attacks of September 11," *Public Papers: George W. Bush,* 1140–41.

16. Some scholars have insisted that the war on terror should not be regarded as a war, but as a state of emergency. Bruce Ackerman, *Before the Next Attack: Preserving Civil Liberties in an Age of Terrorism* (New Haven, CT: Yale University Press, 2006). An emergency regime also assumes a suspension of usual rules, with the difficult question of who has the power to decide when the suspension of the rule of law should come to an end. See generally Kim Lane Scheppele, "Law in a Time of Emergency: States of Exception and the Temptations of 9/11," *University of Pennsylvania Journal of Constitutional Law* 6 (2004): 1001–83.

17. Richard A. Clarke, *Against All Enemies: Inside America's War on Terror* (New York: Free Press, 2004), 24; Michael Otterman, *American Torture: From the Cold War to Abu Ghraib and Beyond* (Melbourne: Melbourne University Press, 2007), 117.

18. Authorization for Use of Military Force, September 18, 2001, Public Law 107–40 [S. J. Res. 23].

19. James Risen and Eric Lichtblau, "Bush Lets U.S. Spy on Callers without Courts," *New York Times*, December 16, 2005; William E. Moschella to Pat Roberts, John D. Rockefeller IV, Peter Hoekstra, and Jane Harman, Senate Select Committee on Intelligence, December 22, 2005, news.findlaw.com/hdocs/docs/nsa/dojnsa122205ltr.pdf.

20. John C. Yoo, Memorandum for William J. Haynes IT, General Counsel of the Department of Defense, Re: Military Interrogation of Alien Unlawful Combatants Held Outside the United States, March 14, 2003, http://graphics8.nytimes.com/packages/pdf/national/OLC_Memo1.pdf; Marty Lederman, "[Post No. 1] The March 2003 Yoo Memo Emerges! (not an April Fool's Joke): The Torture Memo to Top All Torture Memos," April 1, 2003, Balkanization, http://balkin.blogspot.com/2008/04/march-2003-yoo-memo-emerges-not-april.html. See also Otterman, *American Torture*; Mark Danner, "Torture and Truth," *New York Review of Books*, June 10, 2004, http://www.markdanner.com/articles/show/35; Scott Shane, "Waterboarding Used 266 Times on 2 Suspects," *New York Times*, April 19, http://www.nytimes.com/2009/04/20/world/20detain.html; Steven G. Bradbury, Memorandum for John A. Rizzo, May 30, 2005, http://documents.nytimes.com/justice-department-memos-on-interrogation-techniques#document/p85.

21. Yoo, Memorandum for William J. Haynes, 5, 6, 8, 10, quoting William Winthrop, *Military Law and Precedents*, 2d ed. (1920), 788, quoting British War Office, *Manual of Military Law* (1882).

22. Yoo, Memorandum for William J. Haynes; Jack Goldsmith, *The Terror Presidency: Law and Judgment Inside the Bush Administration* (New York: Norton, 2007).

23. Authorization for Use of Military Force against Iraq Resolution of 2002, Public Law 107–243, 116 Stat. 1498 (October 16, 2002); "Remarks to the National Endowment for Democracy," October 6, 2005, in *The Public Papers of the President of the United States: George W. Bush—2005, Book II* (Washington, DC: United States Government Printing Office, 2009), 1521; Marilyn Young, "Ground

Zero: Enduring War," in *September 11 in History: A Watershed Moment?* ed. Mary L. Dudziak (Durham, NC: Duke University Press, 2003), 10–34. For Vice President Dick Cheney, the "war on terror," appears to extend backward in time. He recently told visiting diplomats, "There was a war on in the 1990's, but we didn't know it." David E. Sanger, "Does Calling It Jihad Make It So?" *New York Times*, August 13, 2006.

24. "Remarks to the National Endowment for Democracy," October 6, 2005, in *The Public Papers of the President of the United States: George W. Bush—2005, Book II* (Washington, DC: United States Government Printing Office, 2009), 1521.

25. *Congressional Record* S8398-S8400 (daily ed. June 24, 2003) (statement of Sen. Robert Byrd, "Prewar Intelligence Investigation"); Bob Woodward, *Plan of Attack: The Definitive Account of the Decision to Invade Iraq* (New York: Simon and Schuster, 2004), 1–30; See Mahmood Mandami, *Good Muslim, Bad Muslim: America, the Cold War, and the Roots of Terror* (New York: Three Leaves Press/Doubleday, 2004), 15–16.

26. Walter Pincus and Dana Milbank, "Al Qaeda-Hussein Link Is Dismissed," *Washington Post*, June 17, 2004, p. A1, http://www.washingtonpost.com/wp-dyn/articles/A47812-2004Jun16.html; National Commission on Terrorist Attacks upon the United States, *The 9/11 Commission Report* (New York: Norton, 2004), 66.

27. Mary L. Dudziak, ed., *September 11 in History: A Watershed Moment?* (Durham, NC: Duke University Press, 2003) (photo insert showing Major League baseball player with the American flag on his uniform and helmet); Jack Curry, "Flags, Songs and Tears, and Heightened Security," *New York Times*, September 18, 2001, 15.

28. Paul Greenglass, *United 93* (2006); "United 93," IMDb, http://www.imdb.com/title/tt0475276/.

29. The line was replaced with "Dedicated to the memory of all those who lost their lives on September 11, 2001." "A Flight to Remember," April 18, 2006, *The Village Voice*, http://www.villagevoice.com/film/0616,lim,72901,20.html.

Oliver Stone's *World Trade Center* avoids the xenophobia of *United 93* and generally avoids the broader context in the story of individuals trapped beneath the towers, with the exception of one character, a former Marine, who notes that "this country's at war," and speaks of the need for vengeance. Stone's most militaristic note is the final line, after a remembrance of Port Authority officers who lost their lives: the film was also dedicated to "all those who fought, died and were wounded that day." Oliver Stone, *World Trade Center* (2006).

30. "A Flight to Remember," April 18, 2006, *The Village Voice*, http://www.villagevoice.com/film/0616,lim,72901,20. html. For example, Elaine Scarry lauded their actions as "citizenship in emergency." Elaine Scarry, "Citizenship in Emergency," *Boston Review*, October/November 2002, http://bostonreview.net/BR27.5/scarry.html. On the flight 93 story, see, e.g., "Flight 93: Forty Lives, One Destiny," *Post-Gazette.com* (Pittsburgh), October 28, 2001, http://www.post-gazette.com/headlines/20011028flt93mainsto ryp7.asp. See reactions to the film on amazon.com, http://www.amazon.com/gp/product/B000GH3CRA/ ref=imdbpov_dvd_0/102–0128569–2432119?%5Fencodin g=UTF8&v=glance&n=130 (e.g., "Much of the power of United 93 is the knowledge that while people cannot realistically imagine themselves with the Spartans at Thermopylae or the Texans at the Alamo, just about everyone has flown in an air liner. Everyone seeing this film can imagine themselves among those brave but doomed passengers, fighting with the courage of desperation for the right to get home alive.").

31. Roger Ebert, "United 93," *Chicago Sun-Times*, April 28, 2006, http://rogerebert.suntimes.com/apps/pbcs.dll/ article?AID=/20060427/REVIEWS/60419006; Johnny Diaz, "'United 93' is a powerful experience," *Boston Globe*, April 29, 2006, http://www.boston.com/news/globe/living/articles/ 2006/04/29/united_93_is_a_powerful_experience/. For a critique of the essentialization of Muslims after September 11, see Randy Martin and Ella Shohat, "Introduction:

911—A Public Emergency?" *Social Text* 20, no. 3 (2002): 1–8. On conceptions of an "other" in the framing of American national security, see David Campbell, *Writing Security: United States Foreign Policy and the Politics of Identity*, rev. ed. (Minneapolis: University of Minnesota Press, 1998). On the impact of the way religion has figured in the "war on terror" within the United States, see Margaret Chon and Donna E. Arzt, "Walking While Muslim," *Journal of Law and Contemporary Problems* 68 (2005): 215–54.

32. E.g., Scheppele, "Law in a Time of Emergency"; Ackerman, *Before the Next Attack*; Richard Posner, *Not a Suicide Pact: The Constitution in a Time of National Emergency* (New York: Oxford University Press, 2006); Eric A. Posner and Adrian Vermeule, *Terror in the Balance: Security, Liberty, and the Courts* (New York: Oxford University Press, 2007). A widely presented paper, Lee Epstein, Daniel E. Ho, Gary King, and Jeffrey A. Segal, "The Effect of War on the Supreme Court" (2004), http://epstein.law.northwestern.edu/research/conferencepapers.2004MPSA.pdf, was published under the title "The Supreme Court during Crisis: How War Affects Only Non-War Cases," *New York University Law Review* 80 (April 2005): 1–116.

33. Mark Tushnet, "Emergencies and the Idea of Constitutionalism," in Tushnet, *The Constitution in Wartime*, 45.

34. Samuel Issacharoff and Richard H. Pildes, "Between Civil Libertarianism and Executive Unilateralism: An Institutional Process Approach to Rights during Wartime," in Tushnet, *The Constitution in Wartime*, 161.

35. Benjamin Wittes, *Law and the Long War: The Future of Justice in the Age of Terror* (New York: Penguin, 2008), 8, 12–13.

36. Carl Schmitt, *Political Theology: Four Chapters on the Concept of Sovereignty*, trans. George Schwab (Cambridge, MA: MIT Press, 1985), 1; Claudia Koonz, *The Nazi Conscience* (Cambridge, MA: Harvard University Press, 2003), 49. On the turn to Schmitt, see Ellen Kennedy, "Emergency and Exception," *Political Theory* 39, no. 4 (2011): 535–50; Paul W. Kahn, *Political Theology: Four New Chapters on the Concept of Sovereignty* (New York: Columbia University Press, 2011),

1-8; D. A. Jeremy Tillman, "Should We Read Carl Schmitt Today?" *Berkeley Journal of International Law* 19 (2001): 127–160. On Agamben, see Giorgio Agamben, *State of Exception*, trans. Kevin Attell (Chicago: University of Chicago Press, 2005); Giorgio Agamben, *Homo Sacer: Sovereign Power and Bare Life*, trans. Daniel Heller-Roazen (Stanford, CA: Stanford University Press, 1998). Adrian Vermeule describes the scholarly consensus in legal scholarship on Schmitt in Adrian Vermeule, "Our Schmittian Administrative Law," *Harvard Law Review* 122 (2009): 1095–1149. See also Posner and Vermeule, *Terror in the Balance*, 38–39.

37. These numbers and the chart are based on a search in the *Westlaw Journals and Law Reviews* database. The search was conducted using a common technique for scholarly impact surveys: a search for carl /2 schmitt. False hits were removed from totals. Cites to Agamben also increased, but this would in part be due to the timing of publication of his translations. Many thanks to Paul Moorman of the USC Law Library for help with this.

38. Kim Lane Scheppele, "Law in a Time of Emergency"; Ackerman, *Before the Next Attack*, 56, 89; Posner and Vermeule, *Terror in the Balance*, 38–39. See also Jack M. Balkin and Sanford Levinson, "Constitutional Dictatorship: Its Dangers and Its Design," *Minnesota Law Review* 94 (2010): 1789–1866. Vermeule cites and discusses Schmitt scholarship in "Our Schmittian Administrative Law."

39. Kennedy, "Emergency and Exception"; Ellen Kennedy, "Emergency Government within the Bounds of the Constitution: An Introduction to Carl Schmitt, 'The Dictatorship of the Reich president according to Article 48 R.V.,'" *Constellations* 18 (September 2011): 284–297; John Brenkman, *The Cultural Contradictions of Democracy: Political Thought since September 11* (Princeton, NJ: Princeton University Press, 2007), 59–60.

40. Brenkman, *The Cultural Contradictions of Democracy*, 62.

41. Peter Baker, Helene Cooper, and Mark Mazzetti, "Bin Laden Is Dead, Obama Says," *New York Times*, May 1, 2011, http://www.nytimes.com/2011/05/02/world/asia/osama-bin-laden-is-killed.html?hp; Helen Cooper, "Obama and Merkel Tell Qaddafi to Go," *New York Times*, June 7, 2011,

http://www.nytimes.com/2011/06/08/world/africa/08prexy.html?ref=muammarelqaddafi; David E. Sanger and Elisabeth Bumiller, "Pentagon to Consider Cyberattacks Acts of War," *New York Times*, May 31, 2011, http://www.nytimes.com/2011/06/01/us/politics/01cyber.html?scp=4&sq=cyberwar&st=cse.

42. Joseph Margulies, *Guantánamo and the Abuse of Presidential Power* (New York: Simon and Schuster, 2003), 36; Katharine Q. Seelye, "A Nation Challenged: Detainees; For America's Captives, Home Is a Camp in Cuba, With Goggles and a Koran," January 20, 2002, *New York Times*, http://www.nytimes.com/2002/01/20/world/nation-challenged-detainees-for-america-s-captives-home-camp-cuba-with-goggles.html?src=pm; Sara Wood, GITMO Photos, April 5, 2006, United States Department of Defense, http://www.defense.gov/home/features/gitmo/facilities.html.

43. *Hamdi v. Rumsfeld*, 542 U.S. 507, 516, 520 (2004).

44. *Hamdi*, 542 U.S. at 521; *Hamdi*, 542 U.S. at 573 (Scalia, J., dissenting).

45. *Rasul v. Bush*, 542 U.S. 466, 488 (2004) (Kennedy, J., concurring). See also *Rumsfeld v. Padilla*, 542 U.S. 426, 465 (2004) (Stevens, J., dissenting) (expressing concern about "[i]ncommunicado detention for months on end."); Emily Calhoun, "The Accounting: Habeas Corpus and Enemy Combatants," *University of Colorado Law Review* 79 (Winter 2008): 77–136.

46. *Boumediene v. Bush*, 128 S.Ct. 2229, 2277, 2270 (2008); *Boumediene*, 128 S.Ct. at 2294 (2008) (Scalia, J., dissenting); *Johnson v. Eisentrager*, 339 U.S. 763 (1950); David Kaye, "Scalia's Fear Factor," *Los Angeles Times*, June 13, 2008, http://www.latimes.com/news/opinion/la-oe-kaye13–2008jun13,0,7314680.story; *Boumediene*, 128 S.Ct. at 2277 (Kennedy, J.).

47. Helene Cooper, "In 2010 Campaign, War Is Rarely Mentioned," *New York Times*, October 28, 2010, http://www.nytimes.com/2010/10/29/us/politics/29war.html?_r=1&hp; Javier C. Hernandez, "Planned Sign of Tolerance Bringing Division Instead," *New York Times*, July 13, 2010,

http://www.nytimes.com/2010/07/14/nyregion/14center.
html?ref=park51; Ashley Parker, "Facing Scrutiny, Officials
Defend Airport Pat Downs," *New York Times*, November 16,
2010, http://www.nytimes.com/2010/11/17/us/
17security.html?ref=airportsecurity.

48. Benjamin Weiser, "A Guilty Plea in Plot to Bomb Times
Square," June 22, 2010, *New York Times*, http://query.nytimes.
com/gst/fullpage.html?res=9B05E0DA1030F931A15755C0
A9669D8B63&ref=timessquarebombattemptmay12010.

49. *Holder v. Humanitarian Law Project*, 130 S. Ct. 2705 (2010).

50. Lee Ross, "Humanitarian Group Challenges Antiterror Law
at Supreme Court," FoxNews.com, February 22, 2010,
http://www.foxnews.com/politics/2010/02/22/humani-
tarian-group-challenges-antiterror-law-supreme-court/;
Steve Vladeck, "What Counts As Abetting Terrorists," *New
York Times*, June 21, 2010, http://roomfordebate.blogs.
nytimes.com/2010/06/21/what-counts-as-abetting-terror
ists/?scp=5&sq=epstein&st=cse#mccarthy; Michael Doyle,
"Supreme Court Boosts Federal Prosecutors in Terror
Cases," McClatchy Newspapers, June 21, 2010, http://
www.mcclatchydc.com/2010/06/21/96260/broadening-
prosecutorial-powers.html.

51. *Humanitarian Law Project*, 130 S. Ct. at 2730; *Humanitarian
Law Project*, 130 S. Ct. at 2743 (Breyer, J., dissenting).

52. David Cole, "What Counts As Abetting Terrorists," *New York
Times*, June 21, 2010, http://roomfordebate.blogs.nytimes.
com/2010/06/21/what-counts-as-abetting-terrorists/?scp
=5&sq=epstein&st=cse#cole.

53. "Iraq: The Long Way Out," *NBC Nightly News*, August 18,
2010, http://www.msnbc.msn.com/id/38744453/. On
American casualties after the "end of combat operations,"
see, e.g., "Names of the Dead," *New York Times*, September
16, 2010, http://www.nytimes.com/2010/09/17/us/17list.
html?scp=3&sq=names+of+the+dead+iraq&st=nyt; "Names
of the Dead," *New York Times*, September 17, 2010, http://
www.nytimes.com/2010/09/18/us/18list.html?scp=4&sq=
names+of+the+dead+iraq&st=nyt; "Names of the Dead,"
New York Times, September 28, 2010; http://www.nytimes.

com/2010/09/29/us/29list.html?scp=2&sq=names+of+the +dead+iraq&st=nyt; "Names of the Dead," *New York Times*, October 18, 2010, http://www.nytimes.com/2010/10/19/ us/19list.html?scp=1&sq=names+of+the+dead+iraq&st= nyt. See also http://www.defense.gov/news/casualty.pdf.

54. "Combat Mission's End a Watershed Moment," *Rachel Maddow Show*, http://www.msnbc.msn.com/id/26315908/ vp/38763792#38763792; "Iraqis to Stand Alone," *Rachel Maddow Show*, August 18, 2010, http://www.msnbc.msn. com/id/26315908/vp/38764769#38764769; "Historic Moment as Last Combat Troops Leave Iraq," *Countdown*, MSNBC, August 18, 2010, http://www.msnbc.msn.com/ id/3036677/vp/38763557#38763557.

55. Barack Obama, "Remarks by the President in Address to the Nation on the End of Combat Operations in Iraq," August 31, 2010, http://www.whitehouse.gov/the-press-office/2010/08/ 31/remarks-president-address-nation-end-combat-operations-iraq.

56. Ibid.

57. Thomas E. Ricks, "Army: Ignore Obama's Statement, of Course Combat Continues in Iraq," *Foreign Policy*, Thursday, October 7, 2010, http://ricks.foreignpolicy.com/posts/2010/10/07/army_ ignore_obamas_statement_of_course_combat_continues_in_ iraq; Glenn Greenwald, "AP Refuses to Use WH/NBC Propaganda Terms for Iraq," *Salon*, September 3, 2010, http://www.salon. com/news/opinion/glenn_greenwald/2010/09/03/iraq. Thanks to Robert Chesney for the Ricks reference.

58. Obama, "Remarks by the President in Address to the Nation on the End of Combat Operations in Iraq."

59. Mark Boal, *The Hurt Locker*, directed by Kathryn Bigelow (2009; Santa Monica, CA: Summit Entertainment, 2010), DVD.

Conclusion

1. Franklin D. Roosevelt, "Christmas Eve Message to the Nation," December 24, 1941, *The American Presidency Project*, http://www.presidency.ucsb.edu/ws/index. php?pid=16073&st=&;st1=.

2. Thomas M. Allen, *A Republic in Time: Temporality and Social Imagination in Nineteenth-Century America* (Chapel Hill: University of North Carolina Press, 2008), 217.

3. Richard M. Nixon, "Remarks at the Lighting of the Nation's Christmas Tree," December 16, 1969, *The American Presidency Project*, http://www.presidency.ucsb.edu/ws/index.php?pid=2375&st=pageant+of+peace&;st1=.

4. George W. Bush, "Remarks on Lighting the National Christmas Tree," December 6, 2001, *The American Presidency Project*, http://www.presidency.ucsb.edu/ws/index.php?pid=7 3502&st=pageant+of+peace&;st1=; President George W. Bush, Address, to the Nation, November 8, 2001, http://www.september11news.com/PresidentBushAtlanta.htm.

5. Barack Obama, "Remarks by the President at Lighting of the National Christmas Tree," December 9, 2010, http://www.whitehouse.gov/the-press-office/2010/12/09/remarks-president-lighting-national-christmas-tree; Barack and Michelle Obama, "Weekly Address: Merry Christmas from the President & First Lady," http://www.whitehouse.gov/holidays.

6. John Brenkman, *The Cultural Contradictions of Democracy: Political Thought since September 11* (Princeton, NJ: Princeton University Press, 2007), 60–62.

7. Adrian Lewis points to this problem, noting that with the demise of the citizen soldier with the move to all-volunteer forces, the people were severed from the Clausewitzian trinity—the relationship between the people, the military, and the government—undermining democratic checks on military action. Lewis, *The American Culture of War*. See also Carl von Clausewitz, *On War*, trans. Michael Howard and Peter Paret, ed. Beatrice Heuser (New York: Oxford University Press, 2007), 13–31.

INDEX